Wholeness
Healing From Molestation & Sex Addiction

Jason Thompson

Jason Thompson's unadulterated, raw, and courageous memoir demonstrates the strength of a true man. His vulnerable and lively recounting of his sexual and spiritual journey is captivating. Witnessing him growing, learning, and shifting is a beautiful portrayal of personal power and human resiliency which gives guidance and inspiration to a large number of men who are struggling with sexual trauma and are in desperate need of healing. May this book be the catalyst for men to bravely face their darkness and shift into *Wholeness*.

-- Jessica Smith Relationship Expert

Much has been written about the ability of a memoir to soothe mental, emotional and spiritual wounds of the past. *Wholeness: Healing From Molestation & Sex Addiction*, is no different. This book is a front row seat to a journey through the resilient eyes of a child as he transforms into a gifted healer, author, entrepreneur and family man. Travel with Jason Thompson as he navigates growing up Black in a middle class American family on the eastern plains of suburban Colorado. His personal metamorphoses occurs amidst the usual coming of age complexities framed by ADHD, religious, and social struggles. The hidden burden of sexual trauma, adds a layer of self-alienation and disillusionment that threatens everything until introspection, faith, courage and a willingness to face his own truth allows him to heal while holding nothing back.

-- Anne Garrett-Mills, MD

Wholeness: Healing From Molestation &Sex Addiction ISBN: 978-1-7324519-2-6

© 2021 by Jason Thompson

All scripture references are from the *Bible In Basic English*, 1965, Cambridge Press.

PRINTED IN THE UNITED STATES OF AMERICA

Table of Contents

Dedication

This is a letter to all of the boys and men in the world who have suffered or are suffering from molestation and sex addiction. To all of these silent male voices in the world...*this is for you.*

Preface

The message I want to hit home is sexual molestation happens to boys, just like it happens to girls. I did not realize its effect on me until I was 24 years old. My wounds from that experience were revealed through my addiction to sex and women, that grew more *intense* with each passing year.

It took me six more years from then to *sever my* sex ties with other women and another two years to make the transition from being a grown-up boy into becoming a *real* man. From then, it was another two years before my new self and actions came into proper alignment; thereby breaking the old ties of brokenness and developing into a whole person. There was a 13-year stretch when I had no clue of the spiritual damage I was doing to myself and to my sacredness, which prevented me from experiencing wholeness.

This book is the story of my journey to *healing* and my becoming a whole person and a *real* man.

Introduction

As you begin to read this memoir and personal narrative, understand that these are real-life events that took place in my life. Being molested at a young age and having sex at a young age can *impact* how you see the world and the decisions you make from that point on.

We often *accept* what happens to us and "just move on" without actually putting in the time, effort, and energy to remove the fear and look ourselves in the mirror to *reboot* ourselves. We never stop to *deal* with what happened to us so we can become a *whole* person and operate as a *real* man. We "just accept it and move on."

Acknowledge your brokenness.

Make the necessary corrections.

Identify the new you and move forward.

Moving forward means you are no longer spiritually *attached* or *connected* to the *trauma* from your past. This book documented my life's evolution. I desire to help other boys and even "grown boys" who think they are men (no pun intended) to realize that they can be, have the power to be and can operate as whole people and real men. This book will help men make the *changes* they need to *become* the men they *aspire* to be and *prevent* young ones from making unnecessary *mistakes* that will ultimately prove *costly*.

We need *more* healthy men in this world, and it *starts* by having mentally healthy boys, who will eventually become *better* men. Healthier *men*, means healthier *families* and healthier *communities*. There is no reason to be ashamed of *who* you are or *what* happened to you.

Be *aware* you do not have to *accept* it.

Carry this with you for the rest of your life.

I Love You And I Believe In You!

I hope this story sparks or triggers something inside of you. Recognize *what* it is, begin to *unpack* it, get to the *root* cause and address it at its *core*.

Once again, there is no need to be ashamed. You are a human being. What you went through does not make you less of a *person*, less of a *boy*, or less of a *man*. This narrative is not a boast or brag in any way. This book is to *encourage* you to do the opposite and *avoid* the mistakes I made or correct the ones you have already made.

Know that you are *valuable* and *worthy* of great things. If this book *helps* you to get through a challenging period in your life, *saves* you from severe heartache, or even *preserves* your life, then I could not ask for anything more.

Growing Up On Idalia St

I remember one Tuesday night at the beginning of the summer of 1996, as I transitioned from the fifth grade to middle school. I was lying on the *top* bunk of my cool, blue, bunk bed, just chilling, snuggled up watching Fresh Prince of Bel-Air reruns. I *enjoyed* the summer nights that would follow days filled with no cares, intense, competitive, one-on-one basketball sessions, and baseball games with neighborhood friends.

This moment *changed* my summer and the course of my life *forever*. I had no idea of the tremendous *hurt* it would bring my life as a grown man.

That evening had *started* with laughter, as I sat there *enjoying* my late night entertainment. I got quiet as my body and mind became aligned, and I started drifting off to sleep. Right before I dozed off, I had this abrupt question pop up in my head. It did not make any sense. It was out of the blue.

"Do I have HIV (AIDS)?"

Now the reality is, no kid, and I mean no kid at this age, should have such questions flowing through their mind about AIDS.

Well, this particular night, I *did*.

You may be wondering *why* I was asking myself that question? I will get to that shortly. I did not think much about it at first but realized I could not get it out of my head. Then my heart started *racing* as I began to panic. I started having *crazy* thoughts going buck wild in my head, like bulls *refusing* to be tamed.

I turned off the 12-inch Zenith TV in my room, and started taking deep breaths, trying to convince myself that *nothing* was wrong. Nothing I was doing was bringing my little mind and spirit any peace whatsoever.

My *next* course of action was calling my mom.

She did not work or live in Colorado during the week. She worked in Fort Worth, Texas. My dad was fast asleep, though he was not the one to talk to about this matter. As a young boy, I felt I would get comfort and security from *my mom*; she seemed to have an *instinct* for dealing with heart matters.

The phone was hanging at the end of the kitchen with a comfortable chair underneath. I sat in the chair looking out the window into the pitch darkness, trying to keep my voice down so I would not wake up my dad or sister. I began to share the *troubling* thoughts I was having with my mother.

I can still hear the tone of her voice in my head. I could not stop panicking. She was taken aback by my question. What mother would not be stunned? Imagine your one and *only* son calling from another state, in a *fright,* in the middle of the night.

I could tell that she wanted to panic as well; however, she was conscious that I had called her, so she kept from expressing her alarm. If she panicked, we would both lose it over the phone. Her staying calm was important so I could *think* clearly. Without it, I would have gone into a state of horror and spiraled further.

She kept her composure and asked me questions about what made me think I had HIV or AIDS. I could not get myself to calm down. It took me a while to get to a place where I could actually think in order to properly respond to her. All the lights were off except in the kitchen. My dad was a *light* sleeper; however, I do not believe he heard me on the phone that night. Or maybe he did and just kept quiet.

I do not remember all of her questions, but I remember several big ones: Did he cum in you? Where did this happen? Are you sure?

At 11 years old, I had no clue what cum was, nor should I have, let alone what it meant to have it *inside* me. HIV/AIDS was still a hot topic at the time here in the U.S. as well as across the world, and ignorance about the topic was rampant in the community. You just knew to *avoid* contracting it at all costs. My mother's questions helped me *divert* my attention, *reduced* my anxiety, and *calmed* me down a little so I could think and try to make sense of it all.

I asked her if cum was like pee, and she responded it was not. Most kids have no clue about this.

Each of the graphic questions my mom asked required *significant* thought. I kept looking out the window next to the phone for something to *focus* on and keep me *calm*.

My answers were, it happened at both our house and his. Yes, I was sure that he did not cum in me.

These events were *scary* and created a *vicious* subconscious cycle. I will explain later. I could have had her on the phone with me all night just for comfort. I did not want to get off the phone. This was only the beginning of what I would consider the most *extended* summer that anyone could ever have.

A summer that lasted 13 years.

Every night of that summer, going from the fifth grade into the sixth, I could not get any sleep. I *struggled* to play with my friends. All I could think about was that I had AIDS...AIDS...AIDS.

During the earlier part of the summer days, around 10 or 11 a.m., my friends and I would hit balls at the baseball field behind our house with our bats.

We would be laughing and having the time of our lives. Usually, basketball would be on our minds or the main go-to as well, but we found hitting balls of all kinds extremely *satisfying* to our souls.

One morning after that fateful night, I went up to the park to play with my friends. I *hoped* being with my friends and hitting those baseballs, racket balls, and tennis balls across the field would take my mind off the intense situation that was *consuming* every aspect of my existence.

Despite each joke we exchanged between all of us, and the stroke of every bat against the ball, the thought that I had AIDS or of dying in a few months proved just too overwhelming and gave me *severe* anxiety and a state of silent, *internal* panic.

I remember hitting the ball, then walking away from the field with such internal unease as I went home, all the while telling my friends that I would be right back. I ran away from them in tears, trying to sprint home, but I kept *shaking* intensely. I never returned to the field that day or any other day that summer. I even left all of my baseballs and bats with my friends.

Later, they asked me what was going on. I responded that there was *nothing* wrong, yet all the while trying to keep it together. I remember that day like it was yesterday.

Our nanny, Doris, was also our neighbor. She is one hell of a woman. A mother, teacher, and sweetest lady anyone could ask to meet or know. During the week, my sister and I were always at her house. My mother worked out of town. Dad worked four tens, (four days a week, ten hour days) at the airbase, which was about 15 minutes away from where we lived.

Doris also ran a daycare out of her house, so we were there all the time. I was up most nights during this summer period, usually going to sleep anywhere from 3 to 7 a.m., just enough for me to forget for a brief moment what I was going through. One of Doris' daughters would come and watch us in the mornings and hang out so she could watch MTV or BET and make a little *extra* money in the summer. She would come over real *early* in the morning, around 6 or so, and I would be on the couch just getting to sleep.

It took some time getting used to going to bed at those hours. Most nights, I was *lucky* if I slept at all. I slept on a *recliner* or couch in the family room. My sleep habits were terrible, but for some reason, that recliner and couch brought some *peace* to me internally, so I could at least relax a little.

I could only go to my room during the daytime because the night *fueled* the already massive fire in my mind. It was important to me that I stayed *clear* of that room at night.

That struggle lasted for about *three* months.

When I was in third grade, I picked up skateboarding, as *many* kids did in the early '90s. There were a few kids I saw in my neighborhood that *loved* skateboarding too. Initially, I was not friends with any of them, but I noticed them and tried to do a few of the tricks I saw them doing.

An Asian family with three high school kids lived on the cul-de-sac, one suburban block over from us. I thought that those kids were the *coolest* thing since Filas or Nikes. I made it a point to *observe* their skateboard moves regularly, and then I would try to do it on my own when no one was looking. They knew how to execute some pretty cool X-Game type moves.

I got pretty pumped up about it when I saw them. In my mind, "Aww yes, I am finna go practice right now."

During this era, I had the typical skater look going for some time. Army pants that were too big, cut at the bottom, right to the ankles, and Nike Cortez sneakers. I wore a long chain that would hang down Cab Calloway style from the 1930's zoot suit era. To top it all off, I wore the King Soopers belts that you would use to strap a kid in on the shopping cart. King Soopers is a big grocery store chain like Kroger.

Yes, that was a *real* look.

My mom and dad were not fans of this look, so I could only wear it *after* school, and once my homework was *complete.* This style was short-lived. Eventually, I started skating in my every day after school clothes.

Another kid, Jeremy, lived at the end of that cul-de-sac, closer to my house. Jeremy and I passed by each other more than I ran into the cool Asian kids. Jeremy and I did not speak for probably the first six months of us crossing paths.

When we finally spoke to each other, our friendship took off pretty well. Jeremy was a few years older than me. He was 12 while I was nine. Jeremy and I became good friends. We played basketball, joked a lot, rode bikes, and skateboarded, more often than not.

There are some details I remember, and there are others I do not. I remember us being "friends" and the *unfortunate* events that happened throughout our three-year friendship. I recall hanging out with him and his sisters, Star, and Joy. I even had dinners with his family quite a bit. The basement was cool looking because his sisters stayed down there and they had glowing stars stuck on the ceiling and walls throughout the basement.

As a young kid, I watched my *first* scary movie with them. I was in the fourth grade. We watched the original *Texas Chainsaw Massacre* together. One would think it was frightening; however, I was not that impressed by it. It was gory, but not scary.

The events that took place, happened in the shower and his bed. He had me doing things to him. These events occurred more often than I can remember. However, I remember only several of them vividly. To some, those events may not seem that bad, but to me, those events and what happened were very *traumatic*. I do not *wish* these events to happen to my *worst* enemy or any child.

It was not until I was 11 that everything came to light. That was when it all ended. Those experiences *stripped* me of my innocence as a kid; however, *overcoming* the trauma has helped me become an *amazing* man. I thank the Lord.

Now, for those 80's and early 90's babies, we had French fries called "Magic Fries." We bought them *frozen*; then we had to pop them in the microwave for a few minutes. They came in a package of six individual boxes. They would come out *sizzling*, ready for your lips to devour. All these fries needed was a little salt and Ketchup, then it was over. Those fries did not stand a chance. We ate them like there was nothing else to eat or as if they were going out of style.

Man, them thangs were good!

Now that I am an adult, those "Magic Fries" are not so magical anymore. There are much better ones on the market. Those "Magic Fries" were a hot item in my house between my friends and me whenever we got together. Sometimes I would have to tell my friends, "Nah, we do not have any this week" so that I could have a few boxes to myself.

Basketball was my *favorite* sport by far, even to the point that my parents had a half-court *built* in our back yard for me to practice. I could be out there whenever I wanted. We even had a bright light with a dimmer so I could play into the night or first thing in the morning. My court was my *sanctuary*.

When my alarm went off at 5 a.m., I ate, I mean devoured, oatmeal or cereal, so I could be outside from 5:30 until 6:15. Playing basketball gave me the *right* start to my day. Even if it snowed, I would take a broom and shovel, completely clear the court so I could get busy shooting and dribbling. Most of the things I did were on and around the court.

I added a trampoline out there so I could fly through the air and *slam* the ball. I ate popsicles out there. I ate dinner on some summer nights. I would talk on the phone holding it in one hand and a basketball in the other. I guess you could say I was working on my one-handed skills.

However, when I went through my *traumatic* experience, that was the one period in my upbringing that I was not on the court much. My mind was not able to *focus* on or *digest* basketball. I was so *overwhelmed*. I did not eat. I did not have a lot of strength to play.

When we first built the court, the backboard I had up was a flimsy, off-white, plastic one. I took $150 of my hard-earned money from cutting grass in the neighborhood and bought a *new* fiberglass backboard with a blue square instead of a red or white one. I was *proud* of myself and what I had accomplished. With what I had bought, I could get *better* at my skills.

I appreciated my parents *believing* in me and giving me something *constructive* to do, making this investment in me and my childhood in such a grand way. Thanks, mom and dad. I love you!

Outside of Jeremy, I hang out with Will, Jordan, Brian and two friends named Brandon. Jeremy never hung out with my other friends and me mainly because Jeremy did not vibe with them. Jeremy was not as athletic, so he lost interest pretty *quickly* when it came to basketball and bike riding on an *intense* level, though he did join from time to time. Skate boarding meant more to him so that was the preferred activity, working on perfecting kick flips and other moves.

An Unforgettable Summer

One day during this summer, everything *changed* for me. It was a hot day outside. We were hanging out in Doris' backyard. We were in the kiddie pool with the other kids she was babysitting. As a small boy, I was able to "fit" in the kiddie pool.

The pool was your typical plastic flimsy blue, with an orange fish drawn on the side. For some reason, I thought I was the coolest kid around this particular day. I had my dad's leather Kangol hat on while relaxing in the pool with my arms draped back on the edge.

Why I was wearing a leather Kangol hat in the middle of summer, I have no clue, but that's what it was for me that day. You really cannot explain a lot of things kids do. As I sat in that pool full of ice water, I realized I could not *shake* the trauma.

I *repeatedly* chanted to myself as I looked over to the backdoor of the house, "God, please take this from me, and I want to forget. God, please take this from me, and I want to forget."

I probably *chanted* about 1,000 times that day. It was not even noon yet. I will never forget it. My heart rate and blood pressure had to be that of an unhealthy, overweight, grown man.

My body language spoke, "I am cool. I got this."

However, on the *inside*, I was crying out for safety and the opportunity to *reverse* the hands of time. I was like someone who is about to take their own life. My legs were wobbly. I had the constant feeling of getting on a roller coaster that was suddenly descending, way before you were ready.

I *dreaded* nighttime like a bat dreads daytime.

Even after I knew that I did not have HIV or AIDS, my mind, body, and soul never became at *ease* or could *comprehend* the negative test result as truth. I still had the feeling, somebody had *stripped* my innocence from me. After this day of repeating, "God take this away from free, I want to forget," it felt like everything *faded* away over a *short* time. I do not recall having too many more bad days after this.

My mom and dad were *past* their emotional breaking point as well, and it was *cutting* into their time alone with each other to *nurture* their marriage. My mom worked in a different state from Monday through Friday. She would have to come home every weekend and continue emotionally *supporting* me in the challenges I was going through.

After a while, that can take a toll, especially on a marriage. I remember my parents having a conversation with my sister and me one evening. They said, "Once 8 p.m. hits, it is mom and dad time.

We will be in our room with the door locked, so do not come or knock on our door. We need time to ourselves."

For the most part, I was able to *respect* that. But I still had some challenges at times. It brought some *frustration* to them, but they were always *patient* with me for which I am ever grateful.

One night, towards the beginning of this whole meltdown, I was on the phone with my mom, lying on my parent's bed on my mom's side of the bed, next to my dad. I was crying and scared out of my mind. I was still trying to get my mind right. My mind was spiraling out of control.

I even asked my mom, "What if dad was touching me while I was asleep?"

That was just *irrational* thinking, and it was not even remotely true. However, when your mind cannot see anything in a *positive* light, you continue to spiral *downward*, and the stories you tell yourself can keep getting *darker* and *darker*.

My dad was a *light* sleeper. He *acted* as though he was sleeping, but I am sure he was not. At first, I did not realize it, but I started thinking about it once I got off the phone. I can appreciate him keeping it together because he could rightly have gone off to *defend* himself or try to make me feel *bad* in some capacity, but he did not. Thank you, Dad.

When I was growing up, my dad was big into fishing. He would be at the lake around 2:30 a.m. and he would stay out there till 6 or 7. Once the boats started to infiltrate the lake, that was when he would wrap it up and go home. One early Friday morning, I was laying in our van in a state park parking lot, right by the lake, while dad had his hook in the water. I was not in a good place mentally. This was when I first started wrestling with my thoughts, so any time I was alone, it was not good for me.

I shouted from the van, "Dad, can we go home please? I just want to be next to you on the couch." My dad was a *nice* guy, however, he did not have a cuddling side. He was a very *stoic* man. So for me to say to him, "Let's go cuddle on the couch" was signal. I did not say it with confidence. I needed him to know what I was needing.

"We will leave in 30 minutes, Jase. Go lay down for a bit longer." That was a *long* 30 minutes. When you are slipping deeper into your dark thoughts, 30 minutes is an eternity.

When I first shared my concerns with my mother, she asked if I wanted to get the police involved. I did, but only to the extent that they took down a police report and *questioned* Jeremy. I did not want to press any charges *against* him because I *still* had to see him around the neighborhood and school the following year and then in high school.

I was not *scared* of him by any means, but I did not want any more *conflict* or *interaction* with him, than what was needed. It took me a little bit of time to think this through at such a tender age, but I was confident that was the *correct* decision for my family and me.

The first day of sixth grade was around the corner and I was very much looking forward to it as most kids were. My parents did fun things with my sister and me, especially with me to keep hope alive and try to occupy my mind and time with constructive and positive things.

Even at Doris' during the summer, we had three hour days of learning...*mandatory*. Spanish, Math and Reading were the requirements during the summer, that way when we got back to school, our brains were still sharp instead of vegetative.

On the first day of the sixth grade, I was *excited* to be back at it with all my elementary school friends. I will never forget the second I hopped out of my mom's black Tahoe with peanut butter interior, to see all my friends standing underneath the tree in front of the school. We *huddled* together, *laughing* like we had all been with each other the previous day.

We stood there like we were not supposed to be there because we were en-route to completely *dominating* the entire Middle School arena. We never skipped a beat.

The sixth grade was a *memorable* year. The Broncos won their *first* Super Bowl. We could listen to music in the classrooms with our headphones on during morning home economics. I even ate pints of chocolate icing on the way to school some mornings.

Every girl I *talked* to was thick and beautiful.

Every girl I *liked* was taller than me.

I had my first *heartbreak* with a girl.

My teacher had dandruff on his forearm hairs. Who the heck has arm dandruff? Every time I was at his desk for him to look over or review my work, all I could see and focus on was his arm dandruff.

I wrote a fictional story about Tupac, Lil' Kim, and Biggie; how they took a boat trip down in Miami.

The whole sixth-grade year, we bounced back and forth between two classrooms that were next to each other. Mr. McDonald and Mr. Hester.

Memorable times.

Brandon, Terry, Cerell, Charity, Ari and the Archeletta twins. We were inseparable. With everything going on in Middle school, I had no time to think or reason to think about the topic that plagued my summer mentally and physically.

The things you encounter in *middle* school are different than in *elementary* school. It is not that you are *pressured* into things as parents or other adults may *allude* to; those things are *abundantly* present all around you. You can find yourself becoming a part of something simply because you have been around it *eight* hours a day. The other kids around you are *constantly* discussing or involved in them. It can be *overwhelming* and subconsciously draw you in.

Nicole was the first one to *break* my heart. It tore me down some serious. We only dated for two or three weeks, but boy was my lil' heart broken. You may be saying, "Daaaannnng, what was wrong with you, boy?" *I was 11 years old.* What do you expect? You learn, let it burn like Usher, and then move on.

I remember most of my childhood like it was yesterday. During the sixth and seventh grades, I connected with and only wanted to be with two girls, Micaiah and Ari. I pretty much bounced back and forth between them through the years. Then Micaiah moved *away*, and Ari went *through* her eighth-grade year before she moved to Atlanta.

Back then, the eighth grade was free rein. In the sixth grade, there were so many emotional transitions happening. *Growing* up. Parents giving you more *leeway*. You becoming more *conscious* of your surroundings. You starting to *see* things differently than you used to. People *appearing* different than they did a year earlier. The jokes becoming more *advanced*, even though they are still simple. You start making more *decisions* on your own. Your parents are there to help with *less* of your day to day decisions, and a lot of them you end up paying for when your parents find out after you get home.

In middle school, you start to *see* girls differently than you did a year earlier, and it can make you *feel* differently than it did a year or even six months before.

I remember sitting in the cafeteria, eating with some friends. They were talking about how cute they thought Brittany Spears was. A girl came by that we have all joked around and hung out with at times during lunch and she commented about giving oral sex. How she wanted to do it to a few other boys in the cafeteria. I told her I wanted in on the action too.

The reality is, in the sixth grade, you have zero concept of what anything about sex really means or the consequences that lurk around the corner. We never did act on it, but there was always the *tendency* to try to fit in to be cool when there was no *actual* peer pressure. Many of these types of situations were all around us in school.

As an adult, you may say, "Wow, I cannot believe I was having thoughts like that and trying to live them out. That should be the last thing innocent little boys at that age should be thinking about."

The seventh grade was pretty chill. It was more like a year of *settling* into middle school. Nothing major happened at school anyway. The one big event that occurred outside of school that year was the Columbine shooting. I remember being in Math class during that unfortunate event.

We had a lot of standardized testing, and I ate more whopper malt balls that year to the point I never wanted to eat them again. I have never liked them since. I gained a lot of weight that year because I was on Ritalin for ADHD (Attention Deficit Hyperactive Disorder) that I was dealing with at the time.

I was almost on the verge of needing to be *hospitalized* due to my lack of weight *gain* because of the ADHD meds. The doctor said if I lost another pound, I would need to be admitted into the hospital until I gained more weight.

The weight gain was a huge *plus* for me. The 50 pounds I put on was *essential that year*. Thank you chocolate whoppers. I played a lot of basketball and kept *developing* my skills. I was *enjoying* just being a kid and not having specific memories *haunt* me at night or anytime I entered my room.

At some point, I did get enough *courage* to sleep in my room without having *unsettling* thoughts, provided I did not rest on the top bunk. The top bunk was where the harrowing thoughts and my realization *initially* started. So sleeping on the bottom bunk was the best option.

By the time I got to the eighth grade, my parents had decided to finish out the basement as my new living quarters. It was a great room with a built-in desk, bathroom, and small living room. Having that room was *vital* to me as a kid and for my healing.

I met an awesome kid named Dre while I was in *sixth* grade. We became the *best* of friends. His mother adopted him. I remember his *infectious* laugh. No one would mess with us because Dre was a *big* boy. Dre was a few years *older* than me; however, we were in the *same* middle school. He looked like he could have played college linebacker for some Division I University.

The first time he wanted to stay the night, I started having a *panic* attack. I thought something terrible was going to happen, so I *declined*. I wanted to work through my issue *properly* with my mom's guidance. Dre was cool about it, and we played till the sun went down, then we parted ways for the evening and picked right back where we left off the following day. After that, we were damn near inseparable.

He was indeed one of my *best* friends. We were *always* hooping and completely just *dominating* the streets of Aurora on foot and bikes.

Sometimes, his parents would go out of town, and he would throw parties. There was always weed there that other kids would bring, but it was never my cup of tea. I had no interest in it.

I will never forget when we went across the street from our house to the gas station for a snack. Dre's younger foster brother, Caz, was with us that day. He decided he wanted to *steal* something from the liquor store counter when the clerk went to the back office.

He ran inside, grabbed something off the counter, so we hauled butts on our bikes back across the street. I think he stole a lighter. We were peddling hard as the lights turned green. We were still not all the way across the street, before we saw cars racing toward us. Dre's brother and I were able to *jump* over the curb on our bikes, but Dre could not. He *slammed* his front end into the curb and *flipped* over the bike onto the grass. Man, that was so funny. I will never forget that moment in history.

Dre's brother, Caz, was bad. It reached a point I had to tell him I could not hang out with him anymore, and he was *not* allowed at the house. I felt terrible for him because I knew that he had *continuously* been neglected and was into so much bad stuff. He *never* had real proper home training.

Caz was just over a year *younger* than I. He was *still* in elementary school and smoked cigarettes on the regular. I believe that he wanted to do the right thing, but had no clue *how* or *what* to do. Dre had a mouthpiece on him as well, so he always had cute girls with him. He reminded me of and looked like a Midwest Biggie Smalls version.

There was an apartment complex in our neighborhood. We would always go there to *swim* and *sit* in the hot tub. They even had a sauna in there too. The maintenance crew was never around, so *anyone* would have thought that we were just some resident kids going for a swim.

Sometimes we would *invite* girls to come with us, and we would sit in there, talk, touch, and make out. These were different times. People were more relaxed from a security standpoint. We were able to move freely. Nowadays, you cannot even stand in certain places without being questioned if you have a "right" to be there.

Being that Dre was a few years *older* than me, we walked to school together while in middle school only to part ways once we got to the school. Each grade had its own entrance to go through.

Dre lived over two blocks away, so he had to pass by my house to get to school. He was always knocking on my door so we could walk together.

One morning, in the *dead* of winter, Dre knocked on my door. I stepped out, then shot right back in. It was so *cold* and *snowy* I had to throw on *another* layer of pants.

As we walked up the street and got *closer* to the school, we saw the snowplows. Not only were they moving in our direction, but they were in the lane *closest* to the sidewalk. We had no choice but to *dive*, and I mean dive, *behind* the bushes up against the fence to protect ourselves. Thank The Lord; those bushes were there. If not, we would have had to go home and start our day all over again. Probably would have just called it a day and not went to school at all. No joke. We continued to school and *thawed out* once we got there.

We had some *great* times together for sure.

When I came into high school, Dre was already entering his *junior* year, and so we did not see each other a whole bunch in school, *rarely* passing each other in the hallways. However, the memories we created in my backyard and the streets we ran in remain *forever* written. They should *name* one of our streets after us. I tell you, those streets have never been the same since. To this day, I sometimes travel through that neighborhood to *reminisce*, but today those streets feel dead, quiet, and lifeless.

My High School Years

I lived on a typical neighborhood block in the suburbs of Aurora, Colorado. I was a *biracial* boy enjoying life as a kid trying to *figure* out who I was. Did I want to be a *basketball* player or a professional *skateboarder*? Do I *play* with my friends or *eat* snacks and *listen* to Boyz II Men until I collapse?

High school was another significant, pivotal time in my life. Some *hated* their high school and high school years; however, I *loved* mine. I went through some notable points of hell; however, positive experiences *overshadow* them even more. Those moments turned out to be even more *empowering* than I could consciously comprehend. Entering the hallways as a freshman in high school can be intimidating when you have other older boys sizing you up. You have to hold your own and stand strong till they get to know you...*simple.*

One Friday afternoon in October, around 1:30, my dad arrived to pick me up for a doctor's appointment we had scheduled. It was always nice when you got to go home from school early for any reason as long as you got *out* of there. The days when you know you "leavin' early" nothing else matters. The only thing you can think about is your departure.

I believe it was a physical exam so I could be *cleared* to play sports that year. I *loved* seeing my dad. I always *enjoyed* riding and being seen in his shiny black truck, decked with more chrome than the law allowed, windows down before we even made it out of the parking lot. His truck was ahead of its time. It was a head turner for sure. When I got in the truck and put on my seat belt he proceeded to load his mouth clip, "Son, there is something I have got to tell you."

Many knew my dad as a jokester. He spun many a fun tale. He made a lot of jokes about the Jerry Springer show. "Your momma and I are going to go on there. I was on there last year."

However, that day, he let the bullets fly. "Son, I am moving out of the house. Your mom and I are splitting up. Your mom is not happy anymore."

I thought his words were *blanks* or BB gun bullets, the "hahaha just joking" type. Little did I know those were *real* bullets that flew past my ears one rapid-fire shot at a time. I kept wondering if this is another one of his Jerry Springer jokes, and he was *messing* with me.

"Dad, are you serious?"

"Yes, Jase, I am." Dang, man we had not even left the school premises yet.

One of the bullets that he let off got *permanently* lodged in my heart. It could not kill me physically, but I can *still* feel it when I make certain life moves. It is there as a reminder.

Later that night, I had a conversation with my girlfriend over the phone after I had just got out of the shower. The lights in my room were off. I was laying naked on the floor on the phone with her. I was like a wounded deer that would probably not survive being hit by a car.

I was *upset* and *angry*, but *sad* mostly. I felt *lifeless*. I did not feel as though I was the reason for the divorce, as most kids tend to. I just felt *abandoned*.

"My parents just gon' leave me like this in a time that I need them the most. How selfish is this crap? That is a mess, knowing I struggle in school. Now they want to throw this into the mix even before I have had a chance to get my bearings together in acclimating to the new high school scene and flow of homework, studying, and basketball."

I really could not understand what was happening. To some degree, my thinking was *selfish*. In retrospect, it was probably for *good* reason I was not meant to *understand* everything that was transpiring.

I *struggled* in school academically. I was trying to figure out this new normal of *less* oversight from my parents. There was more for me to figure out. They were only going to be there for me when I *needed* them. My GPA was *scary*. It was *questionable* if I would even make it *past* the ninth grade. I was *barely* breathing with a 2.0, as I moved through life and the hallways of Smoky Hill High School.

With the *separation* going on, I felt somewhat frustrated and *helpless* about moving forward in school. Our family situation *confused* me as a kid who *needed* his parents to be there for him, just like every child does.

My dad was no deadbeat or absentee father. He just no longer lived with us. He was *never* one to help me with homework because he did not have the patience. The school curriculum had *changed* drastically from when he was a kid, so *none* of it made sense to him.

My mom was *always* there on the weekends, and we talked on the phone almost *every* night. She sent us birthday gifts of cookie bouquets to school that were so dang good. She was very *active* as a mother, doing the *best* she could with what she had.

Having family dinner with *one* parent around was no different from when my parents were together. My dad lived down the street. It was not like he was working late to come home every night and kiss me on the forehead. My mom worked in a *different* state during the week. She was not there most nights, either. My sister and I *mostly* ate dinner across the street at Doris' house. She was a *master* cook.

Doris was a *great* addition to my life. She was one hell of a teacher, mother, tutor, and support system for my family. Doris was *always* there for us and kept it as *real* as possible with us. Thankfully, as the third party in the equation, she was very emotionally *stable*.

When I would have some of my emotional outbursts, she would look at me and say, "Well Jason, that is how it goes. You are not leaving until you finish your homework. Do you want to do your reading in the bathroom where it is quiet or here at the dinner table?"

It does not matter how much you try to *replace* something; the outcome will never change until you *resolve* the *initial* dilemma. For me, that dilemma implied not having both parents at home. They could not be together, so I had to figure it out.

I began to make some pretty *reckless* decisions, but not before making the ultimate decision to be *defiant* and do my own thing.

Nothing is more *alarming* than *losing* hope.

That was where I was at 13 and 14 years old. The lack of hope affects everyone differently. I was not *physically abusive* or *destructive* to others. I never became *defiant, disrespectful* to adults or authority. Instead, I became emotionally *destructive* to myself, therefore I became emotionally *toxic* to girls. That lifestyle did not gain traction until I was a little older, at 17 and 18 years old. The momentum picked up like a Ferrari taking off from the starting line with no brakes.

I stayed out most of the night, *sneaking* into my girlfriend's house and hanging outside when I should have had my little behind *asleep* at home preparing for the next day. I would *steal* condoms from the convenience store in the mornings, once or twice a week. I would then go *back* to my house and have sex with my girlfriend, *after* morning basketball practice, but *before* school started.

I lived exactly one mile from the school. I had a basketball practice in the morning from 5:30 to 630. My girlfriend would meet me at school then walk home with me so I could get changed. We would get busy *before* starting the first-period class. A lot of the days, I would altogether *skip* the first period.

The second half of my freshman year was all about sex and basketball. Sex was *high* on my priority list that year. It felt like *wearing* a new pair of skates or your parents *buying* you a pair of rollerblades, and then you *discover* you know how to balance without breaks and pick up speed without falling over.

Having to visit my dad at his new apartment was not fun, and it was a *massive* shift for us all. My sister and I had to make the best of it. My mom and dad decided that it would be *best* if he lived close enough so if my sister or I *needed* something, or an emergency happened, he would not be too far. He moved precisely one mile from our house, which put him *two* miles away from our high school.

Life at that age was moving so fast. I really could not process certain things well, so I *blocked* a lot of it out. I found myself hanging out with certain people who were not good for me. This was not so much *in* school as it was *out* of school.

I met this lady named Yolanda, through one of my friends, Tori. I have no clue how the interaction happened. Tori and I hung out in the eighth grade and our freshman year. Then I started hanging out with Yolanda quite a bit too.

As a growing boy, the desire for *conquest* became more prevalent. That conquering motivation *intensifies* as you get older. A lot of this nature can happen without you even realizing it. It is *ingrained* in a man's DNA from birth.

I wanted to *conquer* Yolanda. "Oh yes, I can handle this; I can show her I can rise to the occasion and handle business."

What makes this story interesting is that Yolanda was precisely *14 years older* than I. She was

28 with *four* kids! I was still a juvenile. Not only was this level of rebellion *unnecessary*, but it was also a *significant* part of the pain and suffering my family and I were experiencing. I felt like I *lost* my parents as a *collective* unit, which I did. However, they were going through their emotional mess and trying to *understand* their new way of life after being together for 18 years, and my dad being single for the first time after many years of marriage.

I was *new* to what was happening to them as well as to me. Yet, for the most part, I did not care, excuse me, I acted as if I did not care. I was a 14-year old whose parents were not seeing straight. I was having sex like it was going out of style. I lived in a *great* home, slept in a *comfortable* bed, had a $75 a week allowance, with the *energy* to play basketball to no end among great friends.

So, what did I feel like I had to lose?

I felt I could do no wrong, *so I kept going*. Given the Russian roulette, I was now playing with my life; I *resisted* any forces pulling me in a more *positive* direction. I *ignored* any attempts to *stop* my *destructive* habits, for the most part.

I was going in hard with Yolanda. It got to the point that she would *pay* for my cab rides to visit her. When I was growing up, cabs were our version of an Uber or Lyft. At the time, she lived 11 miles away from me. I only visited her at *night* or when her kids were *out* with their dad. This story sounds crazy because it is! Too crazy to make up.

Some aspects of my life were a big blur because I was moving real fast, real fast to nowhere. I do remember being over at her house one night. Her mother was there as well. We were hanging out playing a board game of some kind. I got up to leave because I was set to meet some other friends for the remainder of that night.

Before leaving, I had to get something from Yolanda's room. Her mom said to me, "You sure do have the right lips for giving a woman oral sex." She gave me the sign with her fingers to demonstrate oral sex on a woman.

At the time, I thought it was funny. I was even proud of it. I thought to myself, "My parents knew what they were doing when they made me."

That night I knew that I had to *leave* Yolanda and her mom *alone*. That comment whipped out of her mouth like a master *cracking* the whip at a slave.

At that age, it felt bizarre for this old lady on oxygen, barely able to breathe, to be talking to a 14-year-old like that. Her actions blew my mind. I realized I could not continue with some of the activities I was dabbling in. They were the *opposite* of what my parents had tried to instill in me. Discipline, love, communication values, not hanging out with the wrong people, being wise, and so on.

At this point, my life was becoming overwhelming. I knew I had to *change* gears. My memory of this is crystal clear. It was on March 17th. I stood by the edge of my dinner table, and I said to myself, "Okay, Jason, you have got to make some changes."

I called Yo and told her we could not continue our relationship. She *understood* my point of view and was cool with it. I was relieved that we *closed* that chapter together. That stress was no longer on my 14-year-old shoulders. I had no business living in that way.

I Need To Get To Church

I *called* my dad and said to him, "I need you to take me to a church where I can feel alive."

I grew up Catholic until my parents' divorce.

The church we went to was not *alive*. God's Presence was *not* there. I can tell you that much for sure. *Stand* up...*sit* down...*stand* up...*sit* down was the *system* for the church. I *hated* it. I kept falling asleep. There was even one year I blacked out during a Christmas Eve service.

How does that even happen? Well, it *happened*.

I could not let that occur ever *again*.

My dad *found* a church for us to go to, and it was a game-changer from that point on. Heritage Christian Center became my *new* church home. Nowadays, it is The Potters House by Bishop T.D. Jakes. To most, it would have been not only overwhelming but also a culture shock.

I felt like I was *home*.

Loud music.

Elevation of our spiritual lives.

Great voices singing praise to The Most High.

People showing up in their best Sunday attire.

The whole *vibration* of the church was far more *intense and alive* than I had ever felt.

Every Sunday, my dad, my friend Brandon and myself attended *without* fail. It was a *great* way to set up the new week and wash off the previous week's care. It was at this church where I began to *find* God and *develop* a relationship with Him. It was the *first* time The Bible started to actually make *sense*. Like a William Shakespeare flow turned into Tupac mixed with Keith Sweat, "Ohhh, I get it now. That is what God is saying in this scripture? Oh, okay, yeah, I can get with that."

We sat in the *same* seats every week without fail. It was kind of like going to the movies when you are the *only* one in the theatre, and you get to *pick* the seat you want. My dad had a thing about being early. If you were *five* minutes early you were still *late*. If you showed up an *hour* early you were on *time*. We would get there *early*, then quietly *observe* everyone else coming in and *choosing* their spot to hear the sermon.

As time went on, I began to find The Word of God *seeping* into my spirit. The Lord's Voice became *louder* and *louder*. My habits and the way I was thinking and interacting with people began to *change*.

I was *growing*.

Life was *great*.

I got a *new* Jeep for Christmas, 13 months *before* my 16th birthday. It was a gift from my mom.

Mom had a Tahoe, and dad had the big black truck that I previously mentioned. I still have it parked in my garage to this day. Learning how to drive *both* of those vehicles was a *slight* challenge. I could now begin to *learn* how to drive my own vehicle, so I would not mess up theirs. We lived in the *middle* of town, so I could not go buck wild learning how to drive *independently*. The Jeep had the *perfect* size, color, and functional capability for me.

My dad would come over on Sundays and let me drive to church. When I turned 16, Brandon and I met my dad at church, so we all could listen to the message *together* before the week started.

My Jeep had two, 10 inch speakers and a six CD changer in the back, so you could not tell us anything. We would be blasting Mary Mary, Fred Hammond, T.D. Jakes, and a few other artists to stay in the right frame of mind. We had an absolute blast and looked forward to Sundays as if every Sunday was the *first* day of school coming off summer break.

We looked like we should be in a GQ Magazine if not smack dab on the front cover. We always had on a fly suit or a *walking* suit as my dad liked to call them. It was great *bonding* time and *growth* for Brandon, my dad, and me. We held each other *accountable*. There was just no missing church. That was out of the cards for us. We even found ourselves attending mid-week services. I looked forward to these because there were not nearly as *many* people, which allowed me to *notice* people I did not usually see. We attended the holiday plays, which were a blast to go to as well.

My mom came with me one time to a Wednesday service. I *enjoyed* her being there, but I knew she was doing it for me because I would like it. It was *not* her cup of tea. I am *thankful* because I will never forget the moment she was able to join me.

Loud church settings are not for everyone. I can respect that to the fullest extent. I wish *more* people could *experience* it and feed off that great energy.

The Jeep was a gift because my mom felt *bad* for everything that was going on in the family. She wanted to take the pressure *off* in the best way she could or in the way she thought was *right*, not because I deserved it. No 14 year old *deserves* a Jeep or new vehicle. No pun intended. That is reality.

On the flip side of the equation, I was *grateful* and did my best not to carry my weight unappreciatively. I did mess up from time to time, just as any kid would. However, never driving under the influence as a minor or smoking weed in the car. I only had *one* speeding ticket, and that was about it.

Eventually, my dad could not meet us at the church because he got a part-time job that *required* him to work on Sundays.

Brandon and I *continued* to attend church until we graduated from high school. During this time, I also found myself making a huge *commitment* to myself to not have sex for the *remainder* of my high school career. Some may say that was a crazy stupid thing to do, but hey, that is where I was feeling led spiritually, so I did. Removing distractions was pivotal for the next steps.

I did not stop hanging out with girls by any means; however, I did have to *switch* my thinking and frame of mind. I embraced the thought and stance that I would not have sex with any girl I met. However, I did feel the need to see how *far* I could take it without having sex. Once again, a *challenge*.

If I could get a girl naked the first or second time we hang out with just my mouthpiece, I *lost* interest quickly and made a point to let the girl know it on the spot. I guess you could say that made me a real jerk. I know that was not right, but that is what it was. I found it *entertaining*, and it gave me some personal *satisfaction*.

I knew I was not having sex, but at least I would see some nudity. I was trying to understand my threshold and *push* that line as far as I could take it. I wanted to *build up* that tolerance and self-control. There were times I even *convinced* girls to show me things in the hallways or rooms that were closed off with little to no traffic in certain parts of the school. Some of these girls were just as fast as can be and were up for it no matter what.

Despite my commitment to grow in The Lord I was leaving a door *open* for a corrupted heart. My borderline lifestyle was *grieving* Him.

The Bible *cautions* against living like this.

"That you are to put away, in relation to your earlier way of life, the old man, which has become evil by love of deceit;

"And be made new in the spirit of your mind,

"And put on the new man, to which God has given life, in righteousness and a true and holy way of living,

"And do not give way to the Evil One.

"And do not give grief to the Holy Spirit of God, by whom you were marked for the day of salvation," (Ephesians 4:22-24,27,30).

I met a girl in driving school, and we had a *strong* connection. We hit it off pretty well. She was *fun* to be around. We had a blast talking on the phone and going for walks and occasionally going to the movies. I really *liked* her and thought she was a *great* person. I treated her pretty *terribly* though. I had her sit in the *back* seat while my friend sat in the *front* on our way to the movies. There were even a *few* times we did some things in my Jeep, not sex but kissing and stuff.

One day, I went to go pick her up to hang out.

Her dad *stopped* me at the door and told me *never* to come back again. He was *not* allowing me to see his daughter anymore because of *how* I treated her.

I felt awful for her for many years to come. I did not get the opportunity to apologize to her or try and make things right. I cannot blame her father.

I was on a road of *straight* destruction.

I left the front door, walked down the steps, and jumped back in my Jeep, which was sitting on 17 inch Pirelli Scorpion tires. I went on to the *next* spot.

I *forgot* about it and moved on. I did not take it personally. I did not even take the time to sit back and *acknowledge* the destruction I had caused to her or the *wonderful* person I had just lost. The girl was Ms. Aurora, the *winner* of the teen beauty pageant during that time. I was a *fool*.

I held out strong with no sex until February of my senior year. The struggle was real. I could not *resist* the temptation any longer, so I gave in. Once again, I *became* a sex animal. That marked the beginning of sex becoming a *sport* for me, and not realizing it until several years down the road.

What's Up, Dad?

I *love* my dad.

I *miss* him, dearly.

Before the divorce, I saw my dad do some fantastic things for my mom. On certain nights of the week, he would *paint* her toenails. I would come up the stairs to spend time with them or say good night, and I would find him painting her nails. At the time, I really could not appreciate what he was doing. However, I am thankful now that I will never forget those memories.

Once my parents divorced, I saw a whole *other* side of him that I had *never* experienced before. I got to see a *single* man who was lost and did not know how or where to find healing. He was going through so much *pain* and *hurt* he could not channel it properly. It was *weird* to see him with another woman and *strange* to see him living at another residence.

Every time I would go over to his house, he would have a *different* woman sitting on his couch, *entertaining* him. They would be planning to go out to the movies or play pool together. There may be one woman one week and *another* one a different day.

I was developing as a young boy into what I *thought* was a man, just by my age. I *needed* my dad more than ever to be there for me. I needed him to *guide* me in the right direction. Sometimes, as a kid, you do not always recognize what you need at the time, especially when you are living in survival mode. I was headed down some *wrong* paths of my own. I needed my dad to *check* me and give me *better* guidance than what I was giving myself. However, since he was going through so much on his own, it was *hard* for him to discern what I was experiencing, and needed from him.

It was almost as if there was a *preference* not to have a male figure in my life since it appeared to be more of an example of *destruction* than for building me up. On the flip side, I was *thankful* to have a male figure in my life period since so many do not have one. I will revisit this later in this book.

As a boy, this new normal was in some ways a *fascinating* dynamic for me. When I went over to my dad's house, there were *two* things he always made sure I had; a pound of chicken tenders from King Soopers and a 12 pack of Brisk Ice Tea. These were *typical* treats for a kid in the early 2000s. That was *always* a friendly, comfortable, and consistent gesture to look forward to whenever we visited.

My sister and I would be at his house every *other* weekend. To *kill* time, I played a lot of solitaire on his computer. There were certain Fridays I would walk to his house and blast Tupac during my 1-mile. It was *enjoyable*, but also a time of *reflection* for my young self.

My dad did not know I was having sex at an *early* age, but I *wanted* to talk to him about it. So I *did*. I cannot *recall* the day that we had the discussion, but it was at night. I was downstairs, pacing back and forth in my living area. We had a *great* conversation. I got to *release* what had been weighing on my heart.

Here was one of those moments where I was *genuinely* thankful for him and to have him in my life during *this* time. He shared with me that he *lost* his virginity at the age of 12! When he told me that, I thought, "Wow, I cannot believe it."

If you *knew* my dad, you could easily say, "Ah yea; he lost his virginity at an early age. Hahahaha!"

My father was a smooth-talking, smooth walking man. He *rarely* walked fast. He always walked with one hand *slightly* behind his back. He looked like his hand was too cool for you to see it, or as if he was constantly walking through a crowd of people trying to get by them. It was indeed a sight to see.

The man could spend hours, and I mean *hours*, walking through Wal-Mart grocery shopping. When we were growing up, he did *all* the grocery shopping in our house. That was another one of those *unforgettable* memories. Back then, it seemed women did *most* of the grocery shopping.

This man would talk to *everybody*. It did not matter *who* you were. Yes, a lot of them were women, *especially* the checkout clerks. My father interacted with people in a way I cannot quite describe. If you had met him *once*, you were bound to never *forget* his face or smile. If you saw him walk past you, whether outside or inside, he *always* had on the darkest cheap, convenient store sunglasses one can buy. He made them look like a $200 pair of glasses.

At sporting events, when he walked past you, you would have no choice but to say in your head, "Who the heck is that?"

I *enjoyed* being with him in *public* spaces. It always made me feel *proud* to be his son. He looked like a *combination* of Cuba Gooding Jr., Jerry Maguire, and Montel Williams when he had his talk show. My dad had a way with people, *especially the ladies*. That is where I picked up some critical *life skills* in talking to girls and women.

Throughout my time in high school, I saw my dad bounce around women. I saw no stability with *any* of them. There were so many. One night as I was driving down the street late, I saw his truck pulled over in a parking lot. It was around 11 p.m. I called him and got no answer. So, we talked the next day.

With a smile, his response was, "I got some things taken care of." Now, there is no reason for me to say anything more than I knew what he was getting in that parking lot.

Another memory sticks out for me, and one I thought was pretty hilarious at the time. He *locked* me out of the house when I stayed with him because he had some attractive aide over for a *quick* visit. I felt "proud" of my dad. I was like, "Yo! Dad is up there getting busy. Bahahaha."

At that time, I thought that was the *coolest* thing. However, what was happening was *destruction* before my very eyes. My dad did not realize he was projecting a *confusing* example to me. He, too, was *broken* and continued trying to *fix* his pain through sex with *random* women.

I began to develop a *false* reality of how relationships with women should be. I had no example of a *healthy* teenage relationship. It was crazy. At the time, I did not know the *difference* between right and wrong, and quite frankly, neither did my father.

Consider the words of Jesus. "Is it possible for one blind man to be guide to another? will they not go falling together into a hole?" (Luke 6:39).

I am not making excuses for him by any means, but that was what I saw and experienced. I genuinely believe he was doing the *best* he could, considering his *broken* spirit and heart and trying to build a *new* life independently.

It got to the point, when he and I were in the *same* room, sex was the *main* point of our conversations. Who was doing who? How *good* it was. It was a *peculiar* relationship and dynamic. It was a *focal* point that gave us a bond and connection, where neither one of us had to go deep or talk about other real-life situations.

At this point in my young life, I was no longer *concerned* if I had HIV or AIDS. That was ironic. To stay on top of things, I *frequently* made trips to Kaiser Permanente to get tested. The results did not scare or caution me but *empowered* me. I was no longer *thinking* about the trauma that happened to me as a kid. When I was in high school, I went to see my doctor *three* times. Every time everything came out on the up and up.

I was using protection every time, but *sometimes* a condom broke at the last second. I was not sure of the status of who I was messing with, so I stayed on top of those tests for *peace* of mind. The local Kaiser was a 15-minute walk, a two and a half minute drive, from my high school. I continued doing this through my *early* twenties.

I met someone *special* while my dad was living down the street from us. I did not even know how exceptional until *many* years later. It was a hot summer day in 2002. I called up one of my friends, Candice, and asked her to bring *all* of her cute girlfriends to my dad's pool for an afternoon of fun. I got two of my boys with me, and we had a *wonderful* time swimming.

One of her friends could not swim and did not want to get her hair wet, so I *tossed* her in the pool. It was the most logical thing to do, I thought.

"How dare you come to the pool talking about how you cannot swim, and you do not want to get your hair wet?" That was my thinking. "Oh, you are getting wet today, dang it!"

What else do you expect from a 14-year-old boy who likes girls, whose *only* motive is to flirt and see how many girls he can get to enjoy him?

After swimming, we parted ways. My boys and I went back to my house to continue doing what we did best...*hooping in my backyard*. My friend Candice and all of her five girlfriends went back to do whatever they did best...*gossiping about us boys*.

The next day I spoke with Candice. I asked her a youngin' type of question. "Candice, can you give me a picture with all your homegirls in it?" They were all cute, and I wanted to look at all of them.

Later on, she hooked me up with a picture they had taken at the mall. There was a light pink background. They all stood with their hands on their hips. It was a moment in time I will never forget.

When I took possession of the picture, I put it in a jewelry box my dad had given me for my *personal* belongings. It was a star maker's picture. These types of photos were a huge deal back in the early 2000s. The photographs would be taken with a colorful background that matched your outfit. It was one of those pictures a man takes with his boo, or a woman takes with her girlfriends.

For the most part, you usually do not find dudes taking star-maker pictures together. My dad and I took one of these pictures, rocking our New York gear. It was one of the few photos we took together. It was a *memorable* moment. We did not take many pictures together so it was one for the record books.

I had no idea that by putting the group picture of Candice and her friends in my jewelry box, I would be *writing* my future subconsciously. This will make sense later. After that fantastic day at the pool, I never saw most of them ever again.

Working At The Warehouse

I spent most of my early working years mowing lawns. So I decided to get a job at a lawnmower repair shop. My responsibility was to wash the lawnmowers, remove, sharpen, and clean the blades, and then put them in the back of the shop. When the customer came to pick them up, I would retrieve them. I got real good at it. I was paid $7.50 an hour. During downtime, I would *observe* what the mechanics did with the engines. I developed the skill of being able to overhaul carburetors *myself*.

After about six months of working there, I met a cool dude name Cadillac Sam. We hit it off strong. We went to the *same* school but had never talked *before* this moment, even though we passed each other every day in the hallways. We had the time of our lives working together at the lawnmower shop. The unit we worked in, was at the end of the building strip, so we could zip up and down the back alley enjoying life to the best of our ability as juniors in high school.

We would test out old and new ATV's and go-carts, and we would clean lawnmowers. The new ones were from *fresh* inventory. The old ones were what people brought in for *service*. Working here was the *perfect* job for us as teenagers. It held our attention in the right way and time, and we learned valuable life skills.

After we graduated high school, we parted ways for a short time. I went to school down in Alabama. I did not have much success there, so I returned to Colorado after a semester. The *greatest* lesson I learned is never giving up when things get *hard*, or you get *rejected*.

Cadillac Sam and I picked up right where we had left off. Cadillac was now working at AFW (American Furniture Warehouse). He was able to get me a job there as a furniture picker. We had the same schedule. We would *ride* together most mornings, take *breaks* together, and *party* together.

We both had Sundays and Mondays off, so we *trained* our bodies to stay up Friday night, so we could party *all* night long and still make it to work by 5 a.m. on Saturday. Since we knew we could sleep in on Sunday, we would *drink* on Saturday night as well.

After we got off work on Saturdays, we would go home, take a nap, then get after it. There were some weekends we did not go out after we got off. However, the one *consistent* thing was we could guarantee we had a girl at our fingertips.

Cadillac and I had a *similar* way of thinking and operating when it came to girls, though we had *different* approaches. I was a little more *reserved*. I usually let them come to me. If I knew they were diggin' me, then I would talk to them. Cadillac, on the other hand, was more of a *go-getter*.

I wanted to *acquire* this courage and skill, so when we were together, he would *send* me to the frontlines to meet the girls and round them up for our crew. After a while, it became second nature for me and I did not mind the rejection when it happened. Depending on what we were in for at that time, I would *initiate* the conversation, then go after what we wanted or needed for that night, weekend, or month.

It did not matter where we were, whether at a McDonald's drive-through, in line at KFC, leaving after the club let out, at a stoplight while driving down the street, or on the balcony of a hotel room. There was no limit to where we would find women. This stage in my life *solidified* me seeing sex as a sport, which *excited* me. I felt energized.

Sex As A Sport

February 2004 marked the *end* of my commitment to *abstinence* from sex. It took a lot of *pressure* for me to commit to not having sex in high school. No one gave me crap for my abstinence, nor did they ask. One of the benefits of having a *small* knit circle is no one *cares* if you are having sex.

Kids automatically put themselves in *stressful* situations unnecessarily trying to *please* other kids, when in reality, the other kids do not care at the end of the day. When I decided to *start* having sex again, it was my *choice*.

As a teenage boy, my hormones were *raging*.

Cadillac and I were *best* friends by this point, and my room *turned* into a place for threesomes and foursomes.

Where was my mom during this time?

Traveling.

Working.

Sometimes, she was upstairs *sleeping*.

It was just *ridiculous* what was happening in my head and my room. We never *forced* girls to have sex with us or did anything stupid. Our energy was vibrating sex, and we *attracted* others who were like that as well.

We always spoke *nicely* to the young ladies and women, treating them with *respect*. We did not call them out of their names. That was not part of our flow, our vocabulary, or our course of action, nor what we wanted to be remembered for. I *excluded* all emotions when interacting with these ladies. To me, it was merely an *adrenaline* rush. Say "no" to me. Cool! I was on to the next. No heartbreak over here.

After high school I went to Tuskegee University, a *historically black university* in Alabama. When I got back from Alabama (2 months later), Cadillac was dating this stripper, so we were *always* at the strip club. Some nights, we would get there around 9 or 10 p.m. and leave at 1 a.m. We spent a lot of time there so he could be with his girl.

When she was not on stage, we got to play some pool games. We got stomach cramps from laughing so hard, just off the strength of being closely connected and in that environment together. I even started *dating* a stripper.

From that experience, I learned a *valuable* lesson about what is and is not *essential* when courting or in a relationship. I knew for what I was and was not willing to *spend* money on.

Since I understood *how* to talk to strippers and *engage* with them early, I realized that paying for their services would not be in the cards for me. I cannot understand why a boy or a man will *pay* for a stripper. I learned how to talk to them as *people*, so it *changed* my perception. My thinking was, "Why am I paying for what I can have for free?"

After dating a stripper, I *lost* all interest in dating any others. For clarity, I mean no *disrespect* to any stripper or woman who is or is not stripping. I learned and realized that scene was not for me, and the hype is *overrated*. I still went into strip clubs, but I was able to see past all of the nakedness, glamour and distractions of shiny lights and loud music.

When you are in a strip club, every woman has their clothes off; even the waitresses only have a thong. There is money flying everywhere. Strippers are swinging on their poles. Great rap songs are playing that get you in the mood to *spend* money, *consume* drinks, and "let loose."

All the women are there for one thing...to *collect* that money, *empty* your pocketbook and then go the freak home. When I dated the stripper, I stayed the night at her house a lot of times. We had *conflicting* work schedules, as you can imagine.

She lived on the first floor of a decent apartment building. She would get home around 2:30 or 3 a.m., and I would be getting ready to head out to work at the furniture store at 4 a.m.

When she got home, the first thing she would do is *throw* her money on the bed, *count* every single dollar and do whatever she did with it. You could call it a *ritual.* It was as if *counting* her money gave her the *gratification* or strength she needed to go on without feeling *terrible* emotionally at times about what she did. Eventually, things *faded* between us, and we each moved on. During this period of my life, I moved on *quickly*.

When I was in high school, I met a girl named Dimples. She was a year *ahead* of me, and her brother was a senior. I was a *sophomore* at the time. We had a *strong* connection but could not be a high school "couple" because she and her family were Jehovah's Witnesses. I could have cared less about her parents or what they *thought* at the time. I wanted to be with Dimples, and she wanted it *too*.

Her brother caught wind of this, told her parents, and they put a *stop* to it. A couple of months later, she came by the lawnmower shop where I was working to talk and express in tears what her parents had done and told her. I listened, hoping that I would see her a couple of days later at school. However, after that, I did not see her again for quite some time. It was like she vanished. I was quite sad.

The *next* time I saw her, it happened *randomly* at the mall and *once* more after that somewhere else. So we *reconnected*. We hit it off pretty well.

We started having *regular* conversations, and she started developing *trust* for me, only because of the way I was talking to her and *feeding* her mind. I was not trying to be a jerk or reckless (but I was). I was trying to see how far I could *push* the envelope with her emotionally. It made me *feel* important.

Eventually, she wanted to *give* herself to me. She confessed that she *trusted* her body with me. I let her *faith* in me go to my head and took it to a whole other level. I could not believe what she had just said to me.

I was 23 years old at the time. No woman had ever said to me, "Have my body and have your way with it." I told her I was honored and grateful for her.

It took me a few days to figure out how much she trusted me. I talked her into a threesome with Sam. At the time, I was living at my mom's house. I invited her over. Sam came through as well and the three of us had a fiesta in that basement together.

Right after this interaction, we went our separate ways. I went off to work. Dimples was a great woman, but I *misused* her in every possible way. We continued to stay in touch for a while after this; then I let the relationship go because she had kids. That was a cop-out. I was *scared* to commit. With my issues and insecurities, I ruined it all.

I gave her over to my friend so he could have his way with her too. I was a scumbag for real. Even though she was down for that, I should have shown *her* more respect, shown *myself* more respect, and not have gotten Sam involved in the mix.

I displayed nothing but *recklessness*, lack of value to all parties involved, as well as a *poor* representation of what love and wholeness looks like in every possible way. I should have treated her with more value than a piece of meat or simply an experience I wanted to conquer.

I thought I was *the man.*

I opened a door that should have *stayed* closed.

I should have repositioned myself in her life.

The opposite of wholeness is *lack*. When you are whole, you live more in *abundance* and you do not feel like you need anything need more. When you live in a place of lack, you keep taking for the *fear* of *losing* something or *missing* out.

I reconnected with an old girlfriend from middle school. I do not quite remember how, however I was glad we did. We hooked up in the back seat of my Jeep one night, behind a 24 Hour Fitness Center building, but that did not go over smoothly. It was a complete disaster. Here were two grown and much bigger people trying to make memories in the back seat. We scrapped it and chose to meet up another night at my house.

As I talked this over with Cadillac Sam, I explained how crazy it was that this girl and I had reconnected. We had not hooked up since we were younger, and now the time had presented itself.

We joked between us about making this a more exciting story to share between us. I told him to get into the closet in my room before she came over and hang out in there until it was over. I provided him with fruit snacks and a few rice crispy treats to hold him over.

The doorbell rang.

I told Sam to keep quiet and I let her in.

We went down to my room.

Back then, some condoms were made to numb you up so you could keep going without flat lining too quickly. The condom has numbing stuff on it. They were a big deal and guaranteed to work. I had tried them out as practice once before and had success. On this particular night, I was excited to test them out again and see how well they worked.

Neither one of us could feel a dang thing. Numb was an understatement. We scrapped the whole night and gave up after that. "Just go home," I said.

She was embarrassed. So was I, and we left it alone and never stayed in contact after that. Sam and I laughed about that one for a long time after that.

I do not share this to be boastful. What I want to emphasize is I put people I knew at *risk*. I put their safety in *jeopardy*. I made people feel like they were worth *nothing*. This mindset was *childish*, and no one benefited from it.

There was a young woman named Jazmin that we knew from high school. We started hanging out with her after graduation. She was engaged at the time. We had threesomes with her all the time, to the point she asked us to drive her to her fiancé's house so she could give him his ring back.

We thought we were the best people walking since Jesus. However, everything we were touching was getting *destroyed*, unlike Jesus, Who gives *life* to everything He touches. We on the other hand were *taking* lives, collecting names and *derailing* futures.

We boasted about this incident to each other and some of the other guys from our crew for some time to come. Back then, we thought that was the coolest thing, and it gave us a rush of conquering.

Jesus said, "The thief comes only to take the sheep and to put them to death: he comes for their destruction: I have come so that they may have life and have it in greater measure," (John 10:10).

One of the craziest stories I must share with you happened with Sam one night. As we got our food from the drive-through, we had a cute girl serving us. We flirted with her as she attended to us. We took her number before driving off with our order.

One night, we hit her up for us to get together and have some fun. We showed up at her house, rang the bell, and even knocked on the door, but she was not responding. When we called her, she said she was on her way, though she did not show up for quite some time to the point we scrubbed that whole night. It had gotten too late for us, and we were upset that she had wasted our time. After a while you just lose inspiration, motivation and realize that you can be doing something else with your time. So we left.

A few weeks had passed, and we finally got together. We visited, intending to do one thing; the threesome she craved. Before we got there, she had two or three kids to drop off at either her grandparents or the kids father's house.

As we were upstairs in her room, we played around to get comfortable with each other. Eventually, we were in full sex mode, and then...all of a sudden, all we could hear was a shout, "Hey! Hey! Stop all that f**kin' up there. What the heck is y'all doing up there?"

I was taken aback by this. Shoot, we all were.

Sam and I were dumbfounded at first, yet upset that we were being interrupted by another male voice in the house. "Go back down stairs," she said.

She quickly uttered, "That's my dad!"

"Dad, go downstairs," she yelled out to him again.

I shouted from the bed, "Go back downstairs!"

He kept yelling at the top of his lungs.

Finally, I had had it. I walked out of the room naked, hollering, "We are busy up here, taking care of some business. Go back downstairs." After we were all finished, we packed up and told her to get her dad out of her house.

These stories are not to *impress* or *boast*. The amount of spiritual destruction we caused to ourselves and others was *disrespectful* and *degrading* to everyone involved. That level of inconsiderate thinking has *ruined* many lives. We were *ruthless*.

That escapade was *risky*. We could have put our lives in *jeopardy*. Her father may have had a gun. He could have *shot* us.

Things may have ended *differently*.

What kind of warped thinking *justifies* that kind of *disrespectfulness* toward the father of the girl you are in the middle of having sex with? How far gone can you get to be *comfortable* subjecting the father of the girl you are with to hearing the moans of his daughter with someone he knows is in it purely for their fun and not for her benefit?

Granted, the girl was disrespectful to her father because she *knew* he was down in the basement three floors down, and we did not. I did not need to walk out naked from mid-stroke to act like a reckless jerk and make a scene.

Who has the balls (no pun intended) to do that?

Well, on this particular summer night, I did!

One night, Sam and I were cruising down Broadway. We had just left a previous event and were headed home. We pulled up to this stoplight waiting for the light to turn green. It was past 10 p.m. We were in a phase where we mostly listened to music that was chopped n' screwed, with two 12' inch speakers in the trunk. We were attention grabbers. At the time, Cadillac was not yet in a serious relationship, and neither was I.

As we were getting ready to merge onto the highway in Sam's Cadillac, sitting on some 20-inch chopper rims, a brand new red Lexus, with park by itself capabilities, pulled up *beside* us. That was the first year Lexus applied that feature to its lineup.

We rolled down the window, and displayed our big smiles. We asked, "You want to trade cars for the night?" It was our way of saying something funny with the least amount of energy that would draw a non-defensive response, yet was totally unexpected. We were guaranteed to get a smile back, or laugh, at the very least.

We flirted back and forth with her, then she said, "Sure!" The light turned green. We went *through* the light, then pulled over on the shoulder of the on-ramp to a six-lane highway to make the *exchange.*

After she pulled over, I got out and walked over to her car like I was the coolest thing since ice cubes. I had a flow of *undeniable* confidence. My head was cocked back and to the side. I was wearing Italia gear two sizes too big and matching from head to toe.

Before I even stepped to her car, I knew this was a win, and if it was not a sure thing, then I was going to smooth talk my way right into those draws along with my friend. We knew going in that it was a sure thing. She was giving us the same kind of attention we were giving her. After the swap, we went back to her place for a night of fun. The three of us met two or three times after that.

Again, we were setting ourselves up for destruction and putting our lives in jeopardy. For all we know, homegirl could have been *setting us up* for a rape case. We could have gone back to her place only for her to *call* the cops and *accuse* us of raping her, and the next thing we know, our lives as we knew it would be over.

The wise King Solomon *warned* about the dangers of *seduction.* "With her fair words she overcame him, forcing him with her smooth lips.

"The simple man goes after her, like an ox going to its death, like a roe pulled by a cord;

"Like a bird falling into a net; with no thought that his life is in danger, till an arrow goes into his side.

"So now, my sons, give ear to me; give attention to the sayings of my mouth;

"Let not your heart be turned to her ways, do not go wandering in her footsteps.

"For those wounded and made low by her are great in number; and all those who have come to their death through her are a great army.

"Her house is the way to the underworld, going down to the rooms of death," (Proverbs 7:21-27).

We were not thinking along those lines whatsoever. The only thing we were concerned about was *sex* and the creativity behind it to *convince* this woman to be comfortable enough with us to engage.

She was a grown woman, 20 years *older* than us.

She knew *what* she was doing. The energy you put out there will find you whether you like it or not.

We knew what we were looking for.

As a young man, you see these opportunities as, "Oh my gosh, I can't believe I just did that. Yo, that was crazy. I want more of that...again."

The reality is you may not even be thinking of the possible consequences. I certainly was not. We were *preoccupied* with seeing how strong our game was and how we could get those women naked with our mouthpiece, simply to fill a *void (lack)* that we did not even realize was there and *needed* to be filled.

We did not even think of the *challenges* or possible *dangers* that could be staring us in the face. We were still growing up. Sometimes, even *grown* men, do not *see* the obstacles or risks they may be setting themselves up for in some situations.

King Solomon had *more* to say about this.

"Let not your heart's desire go after her fair body; let not her eyes take you prisoner.

"For a loose woman is looking for a cake of bread, but another man's wife goes after one's very life.

"May a man take fire to his breast without burning his clothing?

"Or may one go on lighted coals, and his feet not be burned?" (Proverbs 6:25-28).

My Cousin From Houston

During the Christmas of 2004, I went to New Jersey for three weeks to see my grandmother. My cousin from Houston was with me. We hung out together. That was a wild, but great time. We spent an *enjoyable* three weeks together.

It was wintertime, so we did not spend a lot of time outside, unless for a *good* reason. We spent most of our time in the house watching the first few seasons of Entourage.

Man, we were *hooked*.

We had some *great* laughs, and my cousin put me on to this *outstanding* bourbon chicken that you could only find in certain stores. I was never able to find it in Colorado or ever again for that matter. That chicken was on point.

It had been some years since my cousin, and I had been back in Jersey together. When we were there last, we played up and down the *same* neighborhood street. We spent *hours* in swimsuits playing under a water hose shaped like a showerhead so we could keep *cool* all day long. My allergies would keep me *up* all night as we slept on the porch.

As adults, we got to see Jersey in a whole new light, *experiencing* it in a whole new way. We could go *anywhere* without our parent's permission. We entered the scene without a leash or chains. We even spent some time in New York, watching the ball drop in Times Square up *close* and *personal* bringing in 2005 together. It was wild to see in person what we usually watched on TV, though very overrated compared to what we actually experienced.

Here we were live and in action, standing to the left of the podium where the whole event was filmed as celebrities strolled by. As a young adult, that was a memorable time for me. I was 18 years old.

One night, my cousin and I were cruising around New York. Something *magical* caught our attention as we went by the Fulton Street Mall, focusing on other things to keep our minds off of the cold weather.

As a certain couple walked past us, we looked big-eyed at each other thinking, "What in heck is that? Are you serious?"

"Aw, we gotta get us one of them."

What we saw was *futuristic*. Something we had never seen before. LED belt buckles that lit up, allowing you to enter a saying or a word that would *flash* across the screen. It looked like the stock exchange monitor with numbers sliding across from left to right on a continuous flow.

We kept walking down the street until we found the store that sold them.

"How much do these cost?"

"$40."

"How long have these been on the market?"

"A few weeks at best."

We were excited because we were one of the few people rocking through New York streets with this cool digital set up. We felt like we were a *rare* breed.

We both bought one each and even contemplated buying several more to take back with us to resell in our hometowns, Houston and Denver, at a much higher price. I was *balling* on a set budget, so I did not even *bother* to purchase more, considering it was another week before I would make it back to Denver. Plus, unfortunately, I did not understand the Law of Supply and Demand.

You will see what I mean in a minute.

We rocked the belts everywhere we went. At that time, I was ignorant. I had two sayings switching back and forth on my belt. "That Nigga" and "Living Beautifully." Now, "Living Beautifully" was my cool saying back then.

"Hey J, how are you doing?"

"I am good, man. Living beautifully!"

People hardly respond to a greeting with "living beautifully." They would reply with, "I am doing well" or "I am good." Those are the most common responses you hear.

"Living Beautifully" got people's attention. Shoot, it got *my* attention. As for "That Nigga" that was just too *ignorant*. It was very fitting for me, given the type of *music* we were listening to and our lifestyle.

I left Jersey for Denver on January the 6th of 2005. As I left New Jersey, the temperature was *below* freezing, I am talking *single* digits. Army fatigue material was my clothing of choice at the time. Camo was widespread back then and in high demand. G-unit and Dipset were *popular* styles. Even my oversized camo jacket had fur on the hood. You would have thought I was headed to war...*a fashion war.*

When I got back to Denver, I got a call from one of the boys with whom I played high school sports. The plane had just landed. I was still in my seat, eager to turn my phone back on. He expressed to me that this girl we used to go to high school with was wondering where I was. She wanted to hang out and give me the time of day.

I was shocked because I never thought we would ever cross paths *after* high school. When we were in high school, we never really *acknowledged* each other. We ended up hanging out, shared some laughs and connected sexually a few times; then never spoke again. That was another display of my destructive lifestyle leaving *abandoned* relationships in its wake.

All-Star Weekend 2005

All-Star Weekend was *less* than one month after I got back to Denver from Jersey. During All-Star Weekend, Cadillac Sam and I were live in action downtown. It was cold as hell outside. I may have had no jacket on, but I was wearing the *only* light-up belt in Colorado.

We were walking down the street headed towards the Pepsi Center, the Denver Sporting Event Center, where all the action was.

This guy stopped me dead in my tracks, "Where did you get your belt?"

I responded, "New York. Fulton Street Mall."

He replied, "I will give you $150 for it."

I said, "Naw, I am good."

He hit back, "$300."

"Naw, I am good."

"Are you serious? Why not"

"Well, if I sell you this belt off my waist, then I am no longer the one rocking the cool belt in Denver. Plus, I would be beltless with pants on that are three sizes too big."

Wearing pants that were *three* sizes too big was the style back then. Wearing tees three sizes bigger with size 38 pants when you fit a 34.

Getting rid of that belt did not interest me because I did not *understand* the Law of Supply and Demand. Being the *only* one rocking that belt in the entire state was *significant* for me...*more important than three bills*. Yet, I could have taken that $300, gone to the mall the next day, and bought me ten regular belts.

As we approached the Pepsi Center, we ran into one of Cadillac Sam's friends from back in the day. We greeted each other. They chopped it up for a few minutes, and then we went on our way. As we continued on our stroll, closer to the Pepsi Center, I said to him, "Yo, who was that? We need to get together."

Later that night, we run into Cadillac's friend again. We offered her a ride home. They continued to catch up. As they continued to reminisce, I got to learn more about *who* she was. Before she got out of the car, she and I *exchanged* numbers. We hit it off pretty well and started talking more often.

Since I was heading to Houston in a few weeks, I did not want to make anything official. I was just *playing* the field, though I was *interested* in pursuing it further with this person.

That March, I headed to Houston, and it was the real deal as always. I preferred catching *early* morning flights to get to my destination as *soon* as possible and not feel like the whole day was a *waste*.

My cousin and I were *fearless* together.

Whenever we got together, we always made sure we did not *stick* with the social norms but did it to the *extreme.* We were all about laughs and creating *ultimate* experiences together. From the moment we met at the airport, we were on the move, non-stop, until he dropped me off at Hobby or Bush International Airport.

I visited my cousin for a week while I was still in high school. A year later, I returned. We were not on a leash as we were the first time we visited Jersey. In H-Town, my cousin had his apartment on the campus of TSU, Texas Southern University, a public historically black university.

This trip would stay with me for the rest of my life because of a series of events. Akademiks jeans, Timberlands, and white tees were the in-thing. That was *all* I packed for the entire trip.

I was not even 21 yet, so the only solution was to get a *fake* ID. It was a *wrap* from there. Two counterfeit IDs for $40 was a *steal*, and I would have enjoyed my money's worth *within* 24 hours. After getting those IDs, it was on.

We pulled up to this club. I got out of the passenger side and posted up in front of the car looking fresh. I looked like I ran the town. We were scoping out, formulating and calculating the amount of fun we were about to have, completely prepared to let this club know who the heck we were.

Before getting to the club, we had stopped at the liquor store, then went back to his house and started drinking there in the parking lot. We had a straight blast in that club and shut it down.

By the time we left the club, it was 2 a.m. I had *devoured* 35 shots. We started consuming liquor at around 6:30/7 p.m., and the clubs do not get cracking until around 10:30 or 11. In Denver, you have to be at the club by 9:30.

You may be wondering, "How in the world is that even humanly possible?" Let me tell you, it *is*. I had a *few* vodka shots before leaving the house, not to mention a *gallon* of water before that.

When I was growing up and playing sports, drinking water was *huge* on my priority list and *still* is to this day. Also, the altitude is much *lower* in Houston than it is in Denver. Denver is one mile *above* sea level. Therefore you get drunk on *fewer* drinks. So, in Houston, it was game on.

My cousin weighed a buck twenty-five soaking wet, so his tolerance was much lower than mine. The cards were in my favor from the jump. That whole night, the club offered *two for one* vodka, meaning you get two shots of vodka for the price of one.

What made this hard to turn down was that the two for ones were *under* $5!! I was double-fisting it the *whole* night. One drink in the left hand and one in the right—*two clear plastic cups.*

We met several girls who were leaving the club, and they were driving in the *same* direction as us. We could not drive, so we hopped in their black truck, and they drove us home.

When I got back to my cousin's place, his roommates were *sitting* on the couch, *playing* video games and *drinking* Hennessey. I was in a *heavy* groove. My cousin was out of it, so he passed out in his room. I decided to drink some more.

I got busy and had *four* shots of Henny.

I *closed* the night out with 40 shots!!

Again, with hydration throughout the night and the elevation change, I was able to pull it off. My cousin, on the other hand, was a different story. I closed my eyes around 4 a.m. on my cousin's floor.

I was wide awake and perked up by 8:30 a.m.

My cousin remained passed out. Since I was visiting Houston for two weeks, I started doing some of my laundry. It seemed very strange to me that I was that loaded, yet here I was feeling *energetic*. The *expected* outcome should have been me throwing my guts up, blacking out, and having a *miserable* day.

After getting my laundry started, I sat on the couch with his roommates, chilling and watching them playing video games. Video games were not my jam anymore, so I was just relaxing, hoping my cuz would *wake up* and be *ready* to hit the streets. He was so out of it. He kept moaning how terrible he felt and that we should call the ambulance for him.

I had never heard anything like this before.

We *brushed* it off and kept laughing.

Cuz *crawled* to the bathroom and *locked* himself in there for about an hour. He crawled out to get his phone and called 911 for himself. The paramedics arrived and picked him up.

I rode with him to the hospital.

He had alcohol *poisoning*, so they hooked him up to an IV for *most* of the day. He checked out around 4 or 5 p.m. We got back home to re-up for another go around. He was not feeling like it, so we chilled, laid low, and rested up. The next day, we continued to wreak havoc in the streets, maximizing the most out of every minute I was there.

The following night was one for the record books. TSU was having an event for all of its students at a common roller skating rink on the southeast part of Houston. We decided we would hang out there for a bit, check the scene out, before moving on to other things. The event was *lively*. There was some *great* music, but we got bored because there was only *eight* of us.

We came up with a game plan of what we would do next. We had parked directly behind the rink in the neighborhood, but it was still a long walk from the building to the car. We were having a great time laughing and talking trash to one another.

Suddenly, four dudes came out of the dark and confronted us. They were armed with cue balls and two guns. A rifle and a handgun. They robbed us of *everything* we had. One of the guys standing next to me got shot in the leg. As they were stealing from us, the guy with the rifle *accused* me of robbing one of his friends a while back.

I will never forget the barrel of that rifle pointed at my head in the middle of the road as we stood under a street light. The dude was so emotionally *unstable*. He was chattering and on *edge*. It was the perfect set up for me to *die* that night in the streets of Houston at a robbery gone wrong. You could have seen me on the *First 48 Hours* TV show. They took all our wallets, hats, and even some of our shoes. It was real that night.

Thank The Lord, nothing else crazy happened as tensions *escalated*. Thank God, the guy next to me who got shot with the handgun *lived*.

A few of the guys with us got slapped and punched in the mouth and face with the cue balls. Thank The Lord, no one's teeth or face got broken. I got so much rage and anger out of that night because of how we were *violated*. They took our phones, hats, shoes, and my wallet at gunpoint. I was *pissed*.

I was replaying that night in my head over and over again. I realized that if someone ever points a gun at me *again*, they had better *pull* that doggone trigger. If not, we were going to fight for them even thinking they were going to get away with "scaring" me. That night, I had a mindset shift. I learned some great lessons.

I had no choice but to call my mom shortly after and fill her in on what had happened. I needed her to wire me some money and figure out what to do about my ID situation. After 9/11 happened, all airports *changed* their security rules and regulations. I needed some form of identification for my flight *back* to Denver.

The following day we got everything situated, and we were back in the streets, putting ourselves in *unnecessary* situations. That night, we found ourselves at a Chevron gas station parking lot, pimpin' outside. If you owned a Chevron, you were doing great in life. Over 100 cars drove in and out, some for gas and others for snacks.

Everything was great until gunfire started.
Again?!

We were not shot at directly, though there was no telling exactly what direction they were spraying those bullets. We had to go *back* to the drawing board and *re-evaluate* the life decisions we were making.

After that, we laid *low* and kept it *simple*.

Your energy is so vital. It is easy to *underestimate* the value and *importance* of your energy and where you *direct* it. Consciously, we were *looking* for a great time; girls, stuntin', being in the mix with a lot of people, vibin' and meeting new friends.

We did not consider the fact that we were subconsciously saying, "at any cost, we cannot be hurt." We were *blind* to the energy we were giving to the environment and putting in the world we were in at the time. It is vitally important to be aware of *where* you are, what *energy* you are putting into the world, and *intentionally* direct your strength.

I returned to Denver with a great story, after having a wonderful time with my cousin. How I carried myself and the way I saw my environment here in Denver was different after that Houston experience. When I got back, the young lady I met at All-Star Weekend was still in the picture.

We hit it off nicely and continued to talk.

The remainder of that year was slightly *confusing* for me. I was now 19 and not doing anything productive with my life. I got a night job at Lowe's. I was kind of on an uphill *hamster* wheel. I was very *confused* during this season of my life because I was walking *aimlessly* without a vision; living *distracted* and pursuing women. So just off of this alone, I was *depleting* my energy. No wonder I was confused and did not have much energy for anything else.

In May of 2006, I was looking for something to do, to occupy my time and put my energy into, so I did some research and decided to go to massage school. Classes were starting that June.

Massage School

Graduation was on December the 20th of that year. Massage School was a seven-month program. It was an *exciting* place for me to be spiritually, physically, and emotionally. I did not know what *else* I wanted to do with my life. I had given up on college *twice*. I had a girlfriend I *loved* a lot but had no real *direction* or strong *connection* with. The foundation of our relationship was always rocky. We were *constantly* on *shaky* ground.

A lot happened to me, spiritually and emotionally, as I learned about this trade. The people at this particular school were very sexually *active* with each other. Everyone was sleeping around, with a few exceptions: those who were *married*, those in *serious* relationships, and the ones who were *pregnant*.

There were a few straight shooters, but it was just a matter of time before they *subdued* to being in that environment *every* day. We had class from 8 a.m. to 5 p.m., Monday through Thursday. On the weekend, we had clinicals. We had to *complete* five hours. I chose Saturdays, from 9 a.m. to 2 p.m. I planned to get the hours in *early* and out of the way.

I was *high* as a kite for most of the seven months during this program. I was high *before* class started. I was high at *lunchtime*. I am not sure what prompted this phase, but I was *fully* invested in it.

If I *passed* the class exams and tests, I would smoke an *extra* fat one when I got home that evening as *congratulations* to myself. That was so out of character for me that I just went with it. I was always on edge and my spirit was never easy.

At the time, I was having some *challenges* with my girlfriend. I got so *overwhelmed* trying to do the *right* thing and *making* money that I ended up living in *fight or flight* and straight up *survival* mode.

I was trying to step into my *adulthood* and have things *figured out*, but I could not. I did not know what *turn* to take or what *move* to make. I knew that my girlfriend was *not* a good match for me, but I continued to *stay* in the relationship. I had some real insecurities that I did not *understand* and was not *prepared* to handle or face.

During those 7 months we were off and on emotionally. We *separated* during a portion of those months, before we eventually called it *off for good*. Since we were no longer together, I slept with a student in the class that was graduating after me.

After graduation, I started sleeping with a few students from other classes who had caught my attention while I attended school. I did not entertain them while in school. It was just too much at the time. Having graduated, I got to *have* my cake and *eat* it too.

Once I broke up with my ex, we did not talk for a *whole* month. After that, we had a *few* conversations over the phone. During an argument, she announced she was *pregnant*.

BOOM.

My heart *sank*. My thoughts were *clouded* and *foggy*. I was still in school. I had to break it off with the other student I had been sleeping with. Oh man, I was sweating bullets. I was talking all kind of crap to myself, and reciting a bunch of *worthless* prayers.

"God, please do not let this be true. Do not let this child be mine. God, I will get on the straight and narrow. Please do not let this be mine. I must break up with her. Next time I am wearing a condom. God, I will not even have sex anymore. Is this what I get for messing around? God, I am sorry. I'm a do right."

The *damage* was already *done*.

You may *know* these lines too. If you do not, I hope you *never* do. The day I found out my girlfriend was pregnant, everything *changed*. My *whole* day got *derailed*, my month changed course and so did my life moving forward. I could not think about my schoolwork or engage in any real laughs with my classmates. I did not eat a thing. It took us a few minutes to get our bearings straight and wrap our minds around the fact that we would be parents *soon*.

While all of this was going on, I *thought* of a time when I was *younger*. I *remembered* a few shows on BET called *Def Comedy Jam* and *Comic View*. I cannot *recall* which show this skit aired on, but the comedian said, "At the end of the day, it is ultimately the woman's decision if she is going to keep her baby or not. A man does not have the right to tell a woman what to do. So woman, what you gon' do?"

The comedian was sharing a story that happened in his own life and turned it into a joke. The way he said it was *hilarious*, though he had a *valid* point in his comically delivered message. There was *silence* the moment the test *confirmed* she was pregnant.

Then I asked her, "So, what you gon' do?"

She retorted, "What you mean, what am I going to do?"

"Are we keeping it, or are we having an abortion?" At that time, I felt that was the most *appropriate* thing I could say or ask. I was not fully *aware* of how she felt about being pregnant or keeping the baby. As far as I was concerned, my question was very fitting and justified.

"Abortion? Are you kidding me? There is no way I could do that. I am keeping it."

"Well, then. Okay."

In a situation like this, a typical question may be, "Is the baby mine?" Depending on who is asking, this may also come up, "How do you know the baby is yours?"

I remember the *exact* night and moment conception happened. Before breaking up, we were at a small get together. We had a lot of drinks. The next morning, while mid-stroke, I asked her if she would have my baby. She said yes, so I let it all go inside. The math added up. The baby was *mine*. I had no intention to leave her *alone* to support the baby even if she and I did not work out as a couple.

I was all in for the little one *forever*.

Breaking the news to my mother was not something I was looking forward to doing. When I finally did, she was sitting on my left side, enjoying a glass of wine after having pizza. I informed her that my girlfriend was *pregnant*, and she was going to be a *grandmother*.

She answered, "Jason, I believe you are going to be a great father. I would not be sitting here or this close to you if I did not think you would be a good father."

I was still in massage school. Nothing had *changed* for me financially. On the *last* day of school, I shared with the class that I would be a father. They were *excited* for me.

During her pregnancy, I started going out a lot on the weekends. I was hanging out even more with my boy, Cadillac Sam. Two months *before* I got my girl pregnant, Sam had shared with me that *his* girl was *pregnant*. It was night time, and we were walking into a party when he shared the news with me. I shared my love and excitement for him. I knew that he was going to be a *great* father and was not worried about him. His girl was a *good* woman too, so I did not have any concerns.

Now, here we were, both in this together. We ended up *leaning* on each other even more than ever before. Having a kid on the way at 20 was no *easy* task. I know *numerous* people have children even as *early* as 15, so I *tip* my hat to all young parents. I have mad respect that they were able to *make* something happen and *push* through.

At 20 years old, there is a lot of pressure to already have everything in life *figured out*, and if not, it feels like you have just to *keep pushing through*. So many things are *thrown* your way. It feels like there is a *battle* in your emotions and brain—*a struggle for your energy*. The media is *preying* on you like you are at the center of its attention.

I grew up in a middle-class family. I was never *required* to do any real *manual* or *physical* labor, however, I was expected to give everything by *working hard in any endeavor*. I learned that was not how things worked on the street. I had been *sheltered*. I had a lot *given* to me.

At home, I saw the *fruits* of hard work. It was not *my* hard work necessarily. I did not have a model to *replicate* the kind of success I was *aiming* for or thought I *should* have.

My vision and understanding of hard work were *skewed*. In the real world, *nothing* is given to you. What I perceived as a massive effort was a *little* bit of effort. Those efforts gained *little* to *no* return. It took me a *long* time to *understand* this aspect of my life. I am *thankful* for the *lessons* I learned and the *cards* I was dealt.

I was going a *million* miles an hour without any *specific* direction other than thinking, "Ima gonna be successful." I had a baby on the way, but I was not panicking or freaking out. I was working on finding a job in the massage industry.

I had just *completed* massage school.

After graduating on December the 20th 2006, I landed my *first* massage job in February of 2007. I stayed there until *late* October of the same year. By then, the company was not doing that great. At first, the business was *outstanding*. Everything was going *well*. When the business started *struggling*, I noticed some *flaws* in their system and felt that it was best for me to *part* ways and move on to the *next* opportunity.

During the pregnancy, I was quite *careless*. I was messing around and cheating on my girlfriend *every* week. Eventually, I started seeing an *older* woman. She was *twice* my age. I felt our relationship was *great* because it was *filling* the void in my life created by the *issues* that were going on between my girlfriend and me. Might I add, it was my fault, because as a man, it is my responsibility to maintain my home and keep things in order. But, because I was lacking, or feeling as thought I was lacking, I was out of order, in chaos, and so was my relationship. I was experiencing lack, therefore searched for another woman to fill this void. When I was not at work or stopping by to check on my girlfriend, I was with this *other* woman.

I spent *most* of my evenings with her.

I had no *understanding* of how to *treat* a girl or woman, let alone the one carrying *my* child. I did not handle *rejection* well. I had the mindset that if she did not want me *someone else would*. I did not know how to *navigate* the *sentiments* caused by a pregnant woman's hormones.

I *physically* checked out.

I *emotionally* checked out.

I *hoped* things would just get better and work themselves out. I had a *false* narrative. If you do not take hold of the issues you face in life, they will work you out instead. I let the situation and tension between my girlfriend and me to do its own thing.

I did not take any real *charge* of the situation.

I knew we did not *need* to be together. At the time, I was scared and *clueless* on how to move forward. I just *avoided* it entirely.

One Friday evening, I decided to meet the *older* woman I was talking to for a night of pizza and wine. First, I needed to stop by and check on my girlfriend, so I went by the apartment to make an *appearance*.

As I was using the restroom, my girlfriend walked in *crying*. She was *holding* my phone. "Is this where you are going after you leave here?"

"Yes, it is. But, it is now clear that I will not be going" was my rude and disrespectful response. I do not remember how *long* we spent arguing or trying to make amends. However, I can tell you *nothing* got resolved.

Eventually, I ended up *leaving*. I dashed off to the other woman's house to *destress* and try to *remove* myself from the turmoil I was dealing with emotionally. I could *always* tell her what I was going through, so I *filled her in* on what had happened.

She *understood* my girlfriend's pain, so we decided to part ways to *eliminate* any further issues. Man, that was hard. I wanted her around, but mainly for my own benefit, though breaking things off was the best thing for all parties. By us staying in this *unhealthy* space, I was *preventing* her from going in the direction she needed to be on, as well as keeping my life *stagnant* and *unfruitful*. She had two daughters, a 13-year-old and a younger one as well.

I went *back* to my girlfriend. I *wanted* us to *resolve* our issues. Well, as you can imagine, things did not get *better*, and they did not get any *worse* either.

Eventually, the other woman and I started talking back up again. There was nothing sexual this time, but we *stayed* connected. After my son was born, I even sent her some pictures.

My girlfriend and I continued to try and make things work. Shortly after our baby was born, she moved *out* of her mom's house to her *own* place. I stayed at her house pretty much *all* the time, though she would *visit* my place quite a bit as well.

Later, we moved her and our son to live with my mom and I. I worked on getting our family *healthier*. What healthier meant was staying low key, *avoiding* drama, and trying to *provide* for them.

She caught wind that I was still talking to the other woman. Once again, here I was trying to dig myself out of the *same* hole, just a little *deeper*. The *pressure* became too much for me. One Saturday afternoon, I pulled my car into the garage, parked, then stepped out of the car to go inside. I went to get my son out of the back seat, however, I was so *weak* from *lack of eating* and *stress* to the point I was unable to. I had to leave the car doors *open*. I just sat *inside* the house and laid down, trying to *regain* my strength just to get my son out of the car.

Thankfully, my mom pulled into the garage about 15 minutes after I got home. I was thankful because I had no clue she was coming home. She could not believe my emotional state. Hell, I could not believe the state I was in either!

Being emotionally broken down to the point I could not eat or drink was *tough*. It was *disheartening* and *embarrassing,* knowing I did not have the physical strength to get my son *out* of the car because I could not eat or drink anything. That was not a good *look* or a good *feeling* by any means.

My mom took the baby from my hands so I could gather my strength. It took a while to wrap my head around the fact that I had *let* myself get to this extreme. Here I was thinking I was a *man*. Yet I was still a *boy* myself. I did not go as far as making a vow, though I made a *strong* commitment to myself *never* to let this happen again.

We all go through things. Sometimes those things can cause us to go into fight or flight mode for some time, without taking control of the situation. We may not even realize it. We think that we are not hurting, yet we are crying out on the *inside* for help and guidance.

I was *determined* never to let it go that far again.

This was a *rude* awakening for me and my own health, as well as the health of *others* in my life. I did not want to let myself *ever* reach a place where I have no *physical* strength to pick up a baby...*my baby*.

When you get that far gone, you *lose* sight of just about everything. You lose sight of *who* you are, what you *stand* for, and what you can *do*. While trying to figure me out, here I was *losing myself*.

Sometimes, the path that initially appeared *harmless* is a highway to *destruction*. In the words of King Solomon, "There is a way which seems straight before a man, but its end is the ways of death," (Proverbs 14:12).

Living On My Own

I had never lived on my own *before*.

I was encouraged because as I stepped out on my own, I knew I would begin to gain some *independence* and some other *strength* I did not know I had but needed to develop.

I needed to *nurture* the strength and develop the muscle of *trusting* and *believing* in myself. I needed to know that I could make it without having my mom paying for everything and providing a "safety net" underneath me. I needed to prove I could make it without the *enabling* of my mom's wallet or her *tendency* to step in when it looked like I *needed* help. It was time I began to see how getting away from that *safety net* felt.

At 22 years old, I was doing pretty well financially. I was working at AFW, making $40,000 a year. I could *easily* afford an apartment. I moved out of mom's and convinced my girlfriend to join me with our son, *so she did*.

We *tried* to get it *right* as a couple there.

It did not take long for things to go completely south. It became evident that things could no longer be *resolved* between us, so she moved *back* in with her mom. We began to raise our son in *separate* homes, which worked *better* for us. What was different this time, I now had my own place, was taking care of all my bills and was doing what I needed to do to take care of my son independently.

My confidence and self-worth was building.

The emotional toll that tension between parents takes on a baby is unfathomable. It is *not* fair. This kind of stress on a baby should not be. Whatever an adult does is out of the baby's *control*. The baby does not get a *vote*.

Babies can *sense* your mood. If there is *tension* and *hostility* in the room, they can feel it. We think "they are just babies or kids, they will be alright." That could not be *further* from the truth. They end up suffering as we do, just on a different *scale*, and for them it manifests on its own in a different *form*.

After she moved out, my apartment became a place for women to frequent *regularly* and *randomly*. I was trying my darndest to get over, not my ex per se, but everything I was going through at that time. I was *determined* to move on with my life. In reality, the actions I was fully vested in were making and creating more destruction than I was *personally* aware.

When we become *careless* in our actions and are not truthful with ourselves, we create a *storm* without knowing it or realizing the *consequences*. I was a prime example of this to the fullest extent of the word.

While I was working at AFW, I met a brutha named G. Badass. He was from the south and had moved up to Aurora with his mother years earlier. I had seen him in high school. I knew *who* he was. He was politicking with the other fellas at school that I knew.

However, G and I never ran in the same circles.

When I saw him working at AFW, we started choppin' it up. We thought the same way and even became like *close* brothers. We did not live far from each other. This time, I learned a lot about G.

My son's mother and I had *ended* our relationship. Avoiding *distractions*, staying *out* of my head, and keeping my spirits *high* were my priorities.

After G and I started kicking it, I learned how to play pool. I became pretty darn good at it. We played several times a week. I even had a pool stick from my dad, though I was not *confident* enough to use it, nor felt I had *earned* the right to play with it. G *encouraged* me until I got *comfortable* with it.

It took a little while though. Learning to play with a house stick first was *more* important. House sticks are the ones that the bar has on hand for people to use. I began to *enjoy* the game of pool. It required a different level and kind of *thinking*—geometry on a new playing field.

When I played pool, I was not concerned about anything else. That is what I liked about it. I had to *focus* my mind on the play at hand and how I would *articulate* my shots. How to mix *finesse* shots with *straight* execution shots.

As G and I spent time together, we opened up a whole new way to talk trash to one another. We would have a few drinks and memorize where the girls were sitting. We knew who was coming in and out of the door.

Almost always, we would *position* ourselves close to highly *visible* spots in the bar if possible, or *choose* the pool table that suited our interests best, so we could look at all the women who were present. We would *assess* if any of them were *worthy* of our time or interest, or if we were going to sit there and impress them with our looks and cool styles.

A lot of my time was spent playing pool and hanging out in bars. I was not there to drink but to *play pool*. The only place you could find pool tables was in bars. There were girls there as well, so they were a great place to pass the time.

My style of dressing started to *change*. I had never worn colored, short-sleeved, polo shirts, and jeans. This style was very different from what I had seen in the past or experienced growing up.

By this point in my life, G and I started doing what Sam and I had done in the past. It was insane. One night, G and I left the club. We brought a girl back to my place. She sat on the middle console between us. She stripped in front of us and had her legs wide open. One leg on G and the other on me as we were speeding down the highway.

G was driving. I was sitting on the passenger side looking and feeling that we were about to have fun with her for the night. We got back to my place and had a threesome. We told the girl that she first needed to take a shower before we did anything.

She showered while G and I waited. I remember this clearly. The way we spoke to her was downright degrading as if she was dirty or unworthy of respect.

You are probably thinking, "Well dang J, you did not have any respect for her." More importantly, the reality is I did not have any respect for *myself*. What was happening in my apartment was crazy. We ran girls through there like a freight train.

When you are *broken* like this, you cannot even *see* it. I thought it was absolutely cool to have this kind of chip on my shoulder and that I *should* act this way so I could not get *hurt*.

All I wanted was to *funnel* women in and out of my life. I was *wrong* to the tenth power. I created more *hurt* and *pain* that in turn caused a *ripple* effect, much *further* than I could create on my own.

I went for a drive once and met two twin sisters who were driving next to me. I started spittin' game to them both as we were driving and pulling up to stop lights, all the while making them laugh, which I was good at doing.

I took *one* of them out on a date to Maggiano's Italian restaurant, but I ended up at my place with *both* of them. While at dinner with one of them, we got on the conversation of all three of us because they could not decide which one of them was going to come out with me that night.

Given my mindset at that time in my life, I fixed my lips to do a dance, "Why don't the three of us have each other? She is worthy of being here with us and I think it will be good for us."

After dinner, I dropped her off at her house so the both of them could meet me at my place later for a night of fun and new experiences. I was always living and operating in a place of lack, looking for another woman to devour to fill that void in my life to give the impression of being whole.

After this night, the older woman I had been messing around with, while my son's mother was pregnant with our child, came back for one *last* intimate hurrah. I had called her up one day because I had been *thinking* about her, plain and simple.

The frequency I was vibrating on was *destructive*, not growing or enhancing my life in any way. This frequency is a *damaging* one. Chasing after old flings and sexual ties demonstrates a lack of growth, with the same frequency *repeating* itself like a vicious circle.

I wanted to *push* the envelope. I wanted to see if she would even *respond* if my name showed up on her caller ID. It had been some time since we had spoken. She *gladly* came over, though we never talked again after she left my apartment.

That was meant for the better. *Why?* The relationship we had developed did not germinate from the *right* seed. It was planted in *lies* and *deceit*, then uprooted, only to be buried again and watered with the same ingredients. I was cheating on my son's mother with her. I kept it going as long as I could. Eventually, they both knew about each other, though not at first.

Years later, I was driving next to her on the highway, and we made *eye contact*, but she was with her new husband or boyfriend. It happened so quickly. I could have spoken to her or waved, but out of *respect* for what they had going on, I just kept it moving. We were both *surprised* to see each other at that moment, seemingly so far from when we *first* interacted.

That same day, right after our *last* hurrah, I mean within minutes, a younger woman, who was always visiting her friend across the building from mine, came over to drop off a new pair of Jordan's for my son. She had *never* met my son before. Her and I had spoken a *few* times outside in the apartment complex parking lot. Her name was T. T. She was an ex-stripper who was trying to make *better* choices in life. She gave up stripping and got a *corporate* 9 to 5 job.

I knew what card she was playing by bringing my son some new Jordans. Why she chose that angle, I will never really know. It was well-played though I must say. By night's end, I had her in the bed too, of which I am sure that is what she was wanting or hoping for.

T and I dated for a while, but it ended up being a *rocky* relationship once again. We would be off and on, *arguing* all the time. No real foundation. I was not doing right and keeping my house clean, so how could it work with her? It couldn't.

A few significant events stuck out for me while we were dating. They had a profound effect on me in different ways and at different periods of my life. At times, I was *ruthless* and *cutthroat* in my language and actions. When it came to women, and even in this relationship with T.T., I had an "I do not care to the slightest degree" attitude.

While T and I were at her friend's house, we started arguing. I do not remember why, other than I know it was *petty*, *childish* and a poor representation of our *authentic* selves. I know I did not like *where* the conversation was going, so I *threatened*, "If you do not shut up, I am going to go in there and have sex with your friend."

She kept going on and on, so I walked right into her friend's room and started engaging sexually. Her friend got into it. T walked into the room, and they started doing stuff to each other. The next thing I know, the three of us were in the bed. One could say this backfired on me. I got my way though.

I am not a fan of how I *treated* these women, or "protected" the *emotional* and *spiritual* aspect of the one I claimed to have *loved* at that time. It was a very different experience. We never discussed it after that.

At that moment, I felt that I had to make my presence *known*. I had to prove *who* was calling the shots. We both knew that things were not going to go *far* between us, at least I knew that anyway.

Our relationship *lasted* for a year or two.

I paint this picture because I want you to understand how *destruction* in a male develops and looks like. We think about *random* sexual encounters as some *great* thing. "Ohhh, I am king ding dong. I am God's gift to women. These women love me. I got what they need."

In reality, we are causing a *perpetual* vicious cycle from generation to generation that fuels the *breakdown* of trust between women and men; the sabotaging of what we *can* be and are *designed* to be as one. As men, we have the *power* to *change* that.

While dating, I did not mess with any *other* female, though I wanted to give it to just about *every* woman I encountered.

A while back, I had a conversation with my mom about the women issues I was having. I *expressed* my frustration and confusion to her like never before. She was putting makeup on as I *paced* back and forth across the bathroom floor (the bathroom was the size of a bedroom). I was under the impression my issues could be resolved *in the twinkle of an eye.*

She *paused* and looked at me *straight* in the face, "You need to man up Jason, and I mean man up." Her exact words from that conversation have *never* left me. I *pull* them out of my pocket from time to time and have put them to *fair* use. I could not speak to my father about these challenges or battles of the heart or flesh.

T and I were doing *okay*, but I was *ready* to go.

I remembered the words my dad said to me as a young boy, while we were in the car riding together. This was what he referred to as "the window of opportunity." I decided to use what I learned from my mom and dad to *resolve* my relationship with T.

I sat T down one night on her couch.

The room was dark, but the kitchen stove was on. It was just *bright* enough to *see* each other's smiles, eyes and the *silhouette*s of our bodies. She was sitting to my right.

I said to her, "We need to part ways. I like you and love you. However, I am just like my father, and I want to have sex with other women."

I was *proud* that we had this conversation in *person*. We were face to face. She *appreciated* it.

"J, I know you are like your father and that is ok. I am sad, but I know you J."

At that moment, I learned that by being *honest* with her and giving her the *option* to keep talking to me, *knowing* I was going to be messing with other women, I was putting the ball in *her* court along with transparency. I gave her the option to choose instead of me choosing for her *without her knowledge*.

She may *cry*.

She may *hate* me.

She may be *pissed* at me.

She may *call me all kinds of names*.

The one thing I will not *lose* from her is her *respect* for me. Mutual respect is *essential* for both people involved in a relationship. We remained friends and continued to talk for a few years after that.

Some months went by, and she moved to Atlanta. I even went down to *visit* for a weekend and see how things were in her *new* city. I was *happy* for her, to see her living her *dream* by moving to Atlanta to *pursue* a few of her own *goals* and *ambitions* in life.

When she came out to Aurora for a week to visit her family, she stayed with me, which was cool. We had a great time. When she returned to Atlanta after her visit, I did not see her again for quite some time.

When I worked at AFW for the second time, I was doing *deliveries* and not picking the furniture from the shelves this time. It was even *crazier* and more *exciting* than it was before. I was now in the trucks doing deliveries. I was never the driver, but the guide and passenger man. While I worked in this position, I operated with three drivers: Frank, Caleb, and Steve.

Delivering furniture was very *exhausting* work because it was very physically *demanding*. Yet, not in the same way as lifting weights in the gym. The patience, movements and weight distribution is a different ball game. I got into *excellent* shape.

The better and more *expensive* the route, the *more* we got paid—the better the *driver*, the better the *territory*. Steve and Frank were A-rated drivers, so the assignments would always put us at $50,000 or more. Caleb was a B-rated driver which meant he got the second best routes based on *efficiency* and *timeliness*.

I was as *reckless* as I could be during this time.

Our routes often took us through the *same* streets and intersections, *multiple* times a day and week, so we often ran into the same *people*, like construction workers, fast-food workers, and city workers. I would often see beautiful women and workers with whom I would crave sexual encounters. For some reason, Colorado Springs was a *popular* spot for these happenings.

On one occasion, a female construction worker was responsible for guiding traffic with a stop sign. We went through her intersection *regularly*. We always *smiled* and *waved* at each other as we passed by. For some of these routes in The Springs, I would be partnered with Steve, while Caleb was on other routes.

Steve was Hispanic and a real *smooth* cat. He also had a way with the ladies. Having divorced, he understood what I was after. Finally, I said, "Steve, I need her number like now. After we finish our route, pull over so I can get this woman's number."

We had a good time after that.

While we were doing deliveries in the *southern* part of The Springs, I saw this *beautiful* woman who was slightly *older* than me. She was in a big blue diesel truck. It was something I had never seen before.

Foreign.

She was black and strong.

I had never seen a black woman driving a truck of that magnitude. I thought it might have been her man's truck, *but it was hers*. That took me aback. I could not *resist* getting her number and *pursuing* a connection with her.

After we started talking, I found out she was an Olympic wrestler, *training* at the Olympic Training Center in The Springs. She *performed* at the 2008 Olympics in Beijing, China.

One weekend, she rode down from The Springs and stayed with me. She had a Harley Davidson motorcycle. I could not believe what was happening. Let me just say she body-slammed me on the bed.

At the time, The Springs had some *intense* energy for me. I think maybe because it was *different* than being in Denver, considering The Springs was a *diverse* environment with a *distinctive* type of people. There is a military base at The Springs, so different people and families are always coming and going through there.

A lot of transplants live up there as well.

One night, we went to The Springs to *party* and have a *good* time. I had never reveled in The Springs before this night, either to party or to really interact with the city. What it did offer was single and married women, who were either in the Air Force or waiting for their husbands to return from a tour.

The possibilities were *endless*.

Another coworker, JB, drove two others and myself out for a *fun* night. As we were at the club having a good time, I saw a woman with whom I wanted to have an incredible experience with. I was standing at the bar, getting another drink when I *noticed* her. The moment I saw her I wanted to *devour* her. The way she was moving and strutting around the club had my *full* attention.

We started making out on the spot. The next thing I know, we were having sex at the bar. The club was not too far from closing down for the night while we were at it, then the lights turned on for everyone to leave.

The type of energy you put *out*, you get *back* for sure. The energy I was putting out was straight recklessness.

Conquering.

Destruction.

Sex, sex, sex, sex, and mo' sex!

When a woman has sex with many men, she gives herself *away* to *each* one of them. The same thing happens with men. We *give* a *piece* of ourselves to *every* woman with whom we sleep. A physical *exchange* of energy takes place. In turn, it leaves us with a *confused* state of our identity.

When you receive this much energy from so many different people in this way, you *retain* and *harness* what you gather, therefore your vitality gets *mixed* in with theirs, leaving you in a *perpetual* cycle of self-confusion.

Who am I?

What is my *worth*?

Where am I *going*?

Am I meant for *more* than this?

A real *predicament*. Not only for women but men as well. At this level, the *constant* need for sex is a *destructive* cycle that *initially* gives you a euphoric, exciting, high of adrenalin. At first, it *feels* good, whole and *satisfying* to your flesh, yet is *lost* after that moment, leaving you feeling empty.

Emptiness, confusion and disillusionment *follows*, but the awareness of it is often *drowned* out by the music, technology, and people we *associate* with on a daily, or even minute by minute basis. You may not even become *aware* of this predicament because your life is constantly *chaotic*.

King Solomon warned, "Do not give your strength to women, or your ways to that which is the destruction of kings," (Proverbs 31:3).

At 23 years old, I had a one and a half-year-old son. I was no longer together with his mother. We had colossal communication issues. I was *battling* a sex addiction, without realizing I had one. I was heading *nowhere real* fast while trying to stay on the *right* path.

Remembering the words of King Solomon, "There is a way which seems straight before a man, but its end is the ways of death," (Proverbs 14:12).

Moving Back Home

I moved back home to live with my mom for a short time to *regroup*. This happened right after my son's mom and I *ended* our relationship. I *broke* the lease we had *together* and moved back in with my mom.

Moving back home was a *blessing* in disguise because I ended up getting *fired* from AFW shortly afterward, as many people did *during* and *after* the recession in 2008. On January 7th of 2009, I *lost* my position in the company. I lived at home for another year before mom *sold* the house and moved downtown. My son and I *relocated* to an apartment.

Living at home was great because I was *relieved* of some stress. I was able to *focus* on my career and son. I had *full* custody, so I made sure I could afford the *right* daycare for him and give him a *great* start in life.

At the *peak* of the recession, I was out of work for three weeks...*and three weeks only*. I gave myself a *ritual* every morning until I *found* a job. I remembered a story a teacher in my massage school had shared of the routine a woman followed until she found a job. For some reason, that story always *stuck* with me.

It was not a marvelous story, but it resonated with me, so I *applied* the principle. In the morning, I would wake up before 7 a.m. I would go for a three or four-mile run, come home, eat breakfast, and pray for a few minutes.

Then I would *think* about the career choices and options I would possibly want to *pursue* next. I would do some *investigative* work on company reviews, salaries, and roles. I would *connect* with people in that field and decide if I *wanted* to go that route. This was a 90 minute routine every day.

During this time, God was talking to me. "Go back and fill out an application at Massage Envy."

So I did and got hired *that* day.

During my three year stint at M.E., I *developed* my massage career. I also found myself very sexually involved with a few coworkers and a few ex-M.E. members that I stayed in contact with after they *canceled* their membership.

G and I were kicking it together tough as nails.

We had the *same* day off. He had Sundays and Mondays off, and I had Mondays and Tuesdays. Every Monday, we would link up, either *late* in the morning or *early* in the afternoon, and hit Macy's for some Ralph Lauren shopping. We would then go back to his place for some Lil' Wayne and Madden game time, mixed with a few Red Stripe beers, before hitting the bar for pool time and more Red Stripes.

G came from a completely different background than I did. He grew up in Savannah, Georgia. He was not a gang member affiliate; however, he ran with some pretty hardcore gang members.

G had seen a lot before coming to Colorado and presented a whole different *vibe* to our area. G *never* left his house *without* his pistol locked and loaded on his hip, armpit holster, or hidden in his front crotch. Whenever he was at his home, he had it sitting *loaded* on the table, right in front of him.

G was in a relationship. We put bringing women home for the night on hold. However, that did not stop us from running the streets at night and having the time of our lives playing pool, eye ballin' everything that came through the door, or getting numbers for back up.

Cadillac Sam and I had a falling out over some *miscommunication* and female stuff. We stopped kickin' it. It sucks, but that is how things go occasionally. To this day, I *wish* we were still close. However, that is not in the cards sometimes and you gotta keep pushing through.

I began riding *solo* more and more. I started making my moves. A lot of my stories intertwine, and events overlap. Be patient and continue to follow me on this journey.

With Sam no longer in the mix, G and I started kicking it every *week*, if not every *night*. I was now *living* at home, *working* at M.E., with *full* custody of my son. I was into all kinds of stuff and *never* sat still.

I *avoided* sitting down to *face* my mess. I assumed that the mirror of my life looked good, so there was not much reason to *gaze* at it to make changes. There were now *two* women from my job with whom I was having a fling: a front desk staff member and another therapist.

The front desk staff member and I had *nothing* in common other than sex. The therapist and I were very *intimate* and energetically connected. She had no interest in slowing down or being in a relationship. She was not with other guys, but the *thought* of being in a relationship brought her *severe* anxiety.

She was a huge *flirt* and *high maintenance*. To put herself on ice for just *one* man was too much for her to bear. When we got together, it was highly intense sexually, and we had a great time.

Since we worked together, we kept everything on the down-low when we were at work. However, there was one exception...and one exception only.

There is a saying, "Don't crap where you eat."

Well, I was poopin' all over my table.

A couple wanted to be in the same room during a couple's massage. It was a 90-minute session. The two of us got the assigned together for the first and only time.

On this particular Friday afternoon, I decided I wanted her to give me oral sex during the session we were supposed to be giving the other couple. We were both standing between the two tables as we massaged our clients. We made it happen without skipping a beat.

I could not have been more thankful that we did not get caught. That was a highly *selfish* act and put both of our careers at *risk* with the possibility of *branding* the entire company and organization with a *lousy* reputation.

However, at the time, the *perceived* thrill and rush of having this done during a couple's massage was just too much for me to pass up. We never did anything like that again at work.

The front desk member and I were pretty straight forward. We had an understanding, and it was purely sexual. We spoke at work, but nothing emotional or anything other than work stuff.

She would come over to my house on her days or mornings off. I told her that she could not come up my stairs wearing any clothes. "When you hit this bedroom door, I want you naked and ready."

My mom and I lived in a 6,000 square foot house. My room was on the east wing of the house, with an entrance leading up to my bedroom from the outside. When she came up the stairs, she was ready to have some fun. We hooked up a handful of times, and that was it.

Perhaps you are thinking, "Oh man, you were doing big things. Getting it in, getting all the women a man could ask for."

That would be a *typical* reaction from a *boy*. The *correct* way to describe how I was living is *destruction*. At the time, the mirror looked good to me...*too dang good to look at or even notice.*

Yes, homegirl was down for the cause. However, did I need to be the one causing *devastation* or an *obstruction* to the good things she was meant to receive in life?

When a lion is going after the kill, it identifies the *weakest* link. The one that is off guard or not paying attention. I only preyed on the weak...*the vulnerable.* I was *delaying* these women from receiving their blessings. By taking *advantage* of them and holding them emotionally *hostage*, I was making them wait for their real blessings in life *longer* than they needed to.

In the process, I was even keeping *myself* from receiving my blessing because I was holding myself emotionally *captive*, only operating out of *pain* and *hurt* of which I was not even *aware* I suffered.

Yo...that *mirror* though! I *never* wanted to look at it because I did not *want* to see what would be glaring *back* at me.

I worked at M.E. for *eight* months before deciding to *register* my massage practice. I had to go into the bank to get everything set up correctly. The bank teller and I always had great two to five minute conversations. Whenever I went in to do some transactions, there would always be someone in line behind me.

However, on this occasion, I was going in to set up my business account. That day, as we were setting everything up, the two of us flirted a little differently. I walked out with her phone number and hit her up either later that evening or week.

Before long, I had her in the same situation as the front desk staff member. I had her coming up the stairs, ready for fun before even seeing her. When she hit the door, I told her that was how I wanted her to be. "We are not here for amazing conversation and storytelling. We about to tell these sheets a story of our own."

My actions *amplified* the conversation that was going on in my head. I set the *expectation* for what I wanted; that way, there were no *misconceptions* of what was about to happen or would continue to happen. She was not in rotation long. After a few times, it was *over*.

As you can imagine, the extent of my *dominating* nature did not serve me well. People like to interact, to have an *exchange*. However, a relationship will always be short-lived when it is *one-sided* and *dies* even before it can get started.

When two people are talking, both parties *want* and need to *know* they are involved in the conversation. When one person *hijacks* dialogue, it is no longer an exchange but more of a *projection* from one to the other, with the other person never feeling they are a *part* of it in any way.

Inevitably, they *lose* interest and keep it moving. That was the story of my sexual experiences. The other therapist knew what I had going on, and I did with her too. We just kept it real like that with one another. For her to get upset or even try to keep me in check would go *against* everything she believed or operated in at that time. I let her be because when she and I came together, we knew what it was about.

As time went on, I learned she was using *drugs* other than smoking weed. After that, I left her alone. We got into an argument that made us both take the step to end it, but for *differing* reasons.

She wanted to be able to do *whatever* she wanted. Conversely, I did *not* want to be involved in her actions. I was *hurt* she was engaged in such activities. I knew she was better than that, but could not *force* anything on her. So, we naturally *distanced* ourselves from each other.

We still had to *work* together; but we did not talk as before. Nevertheless, we remained *cordial* with one another.

No Going Back: The Del Arté Years

After we stopped living in the 6,000 square foot house, my mom moved downtown, and I got a different place for my son and me. Everything *changed* in a way I never thought was going to happen.

I moved into the Del Arté apartments with my son. The only woman I still had on rotation at this point was the therapist that I was working with. It took a while before we *stopped* seeing each other sexually.

I was now in a *different* place and situation in life. I felt it was time to find a *new* woman and move to a whole *other* level. G and I were still tough as nails together, kicking it on the regular. We switched up our bar and pool locations. On his side of town, I would play with him and then *return* to my apartment, so I could find some trouble to get into *close* to where I lived.

I never liked getting pulled over or stopped by the police, especially at night. So I made sure I did my best to stay out of sight. I come across a bar called *The Lounge Bar & Grill* located about 175 yards from my apartment door.

At first, this bar was a little *intimidating*. The door and entry point were located so that *everyone* would *look* at you as you walked in. It was always packed...*packed to the moon*. As you can imagine, this new spot became a *goldmine* for me.

I could have drinks, play pool, including great pick-up pool games, and look at the beautiful women all night, all this down the street from the front door of my apartment.

Aww man, this was a win-win-win!!!

What else could a guy ask for in this position?

I was having fun; working, living independently, and having sex with just about every woman who smiled at me.

I kept *mismanaging* my time. During the days I was off, I would spend a lot of time at the mall and with G. So, I found a way to have my manager at M.E. to put me on a schedule that allowed me to work the same hours every day without burning out! On the days I did work, I was less likely to have *extravagant* shopping days, *play* Madden all afternoon, or *drink* Red Stripes.

I did not like the highs and lows of the day working as a massage therapist. I could be on the schedule for the *whole* day, but there would be *massive gaps* throughout the day between appointments or outright *cancellations*.

It put a *damper* on my energy and flow.

I crafted my schedule so I could spend *shorter* chunks of time at work but still get in the time I needed to get paid without *losing* money. The highs and lows of the day would not impact my day as severely. A three or five-hour day is different from being there for 8 hours.

I was able to build up my money *faster* because I was not *spending* it. With this schedule, I had tips coming in *every* day. It was a nice set up that worked well for me.

The Lounge was poppin' every night of the week, like bacon grease on a hot stove. Mondays had Monday night *football*. Tuesdays were $2 *burger* night and bingo. There was nothing on Wednesdays, but there was still a *steady* flow of people. Thursday nights was *karaoke* night. Fridays were just Fridays, though who doesn't come out on Friday nights? Saturday nights was *karaoke* night again. Sundays were *football* days with great *hangover* breakfasts.

There was never a night you could go there and not find great people to be around. On Monday nights, I would be there if I was not with G. Thursday, Friday, and Saturday nights were the other nights I would *always* be there.

When I was there, I always wanted to position myself so that *every* woman who came through the door had to walk *past* my field of vision or directly in *front* of me. I always sat in the back *behind* the pool table, on a bench that ran along both sides of the bar.

I always got there a little *early* so that I could get into my rhythm and flow. I did not like coming in and having to *adapt* to the flow of the bar. I enjoyed playing a few games of pool before the crowds showed up so I could already be in the flow and tone. The Lounge became like my *second* home.

After I was done working or moving through the city for the day, I was *always* at The Lounge. I *averaged* $75 a night on drinks and food. If you found me at the right time, I would be *buying* drinks for people. The vibe and flow of the bar was just undeniably energetic for me. It *drew* me in and had me there.

On the days I had my son with me, I did not go to The Lounge. Each day he spent with me was all about the two of us *creating* fun times and memories. It also kept me *balanced* and reminded me *constantly* what was important. His mom and I would *alternate* every week. He would spend *one* week with me, then the *next* week with her.

I loved *taking* him to and *picking* him up from school, so I made sure that I could do that on *most* days, even on the weeks he was with his mom. Those were *precious* moments that I did not want to *miss*. I also wanted to *keep* the peace between his mother and me. We purposed for our son to see *togetherness* and not cutthroat *division*.

If I *wanted* food from The Lounge on a week my son was *with* me, I would *order* it to take back to the house. This period of my life was a *defining* one for me. It was a process for which I am grateful.

I do not recall the first time I walked into The Lounge or the first woman I brought back to my place. I was never one for going into a bar, simply to sit down and drink. That was never my style.

The pool tables allowed me to *connect* with others, as well as with *myself*. To smile, laugh, scope out the lay of the land, establish eye contact, share good food, and have a drink.

The pool table was a great ice breaker for other interactions and a *departure* from drinking. Drinking by itself can get boring *quickly*. Drinking can also get you into *unnecessary* trouble.

Pool games were a great *replacement*. You cannot focus on the right *angles* for your shots or the ball's *velocity* after you have had too many drinks. I never went into the bar with the *sole* intention of finding a woman to bring back to my place, but it was definitely in the equation for the night.

Sometimes that equation did not involve bringing a woman back to my place, which was fine with me. Before *leaving* the house, I could *feel* what type of night it would be based on my vibe and the energy level I was putting into the evening and night.

Since I lived *across* the street from the bar, it was relatively *easy* for me to invite a woman back to my place. "Yo, I live just across the street. Come over for a lil' while then you can go home."

It never seemed *out* of the way for them to come over. There were other times when the dialog would be, "Slide through for the night when you get off work. I'll be up so just come over to the front gate and I will buzz you in."

Those are not the only words I would say, but they helped. There was less pressure. Often, the energy was so intense, the conversation and interaction wise, that it was a no-brainer of what we were going to do next and where.

Sometimes, nothing would happen on the first night we met. We would meet two or three times before we would have sex, and it would often occur at their house and not mine. Occasionally, I preferred it that way. I wanted to have sexual encounters with most of the women that came into the bar at that time.

My *want* and *need* for sex was very *unhealthy*.

King Solomon wisely said, "Do not give your strength to women, or your ways to that which is the destruction of kings," (Proverbs 31:3).

The Increase

I had no *shame* in my game.

I came home with all kinds of women from The Lounge, even the waitresses. One night, I was at the bar doing my thing, playing pool, laughing, conversating with everybody, moving from one end of the bar to the next, and having great pool games. I started talking to this nice young woman. Just like me, she was in her *early* twenties.

We went back to my place and had a great night.

After we woke up, I realized she was full-blown pregnant. She even had a linea nigra, the line pregnant women get when they are well into their pregnancy, which means she was about to pop right into labor.

I clearly had too much to drink that night. I could not believe this...*I had no clue homegirl was pregnant*. This was an embarrassing moment for me in my life. I remember talking to her, laughing with her and so forth, but I did not see anything that resembled being pregnant while at the bar.

There were many mornings I would wake up, and my anxiety would be so bad I would have to go for a run in the morning. As the women slept, I would go for a quick two-mile run through the neighborhood.

However, that morning, I saw her pregnant belly before I went on my run. I could not believe it. When I returned, she was up and ready to leave. I dropped her off at home and went on with my day.

Later, I went to the steam room to purge the alcohol from my body before continuing with my daily routine. From the time I was 18 years old, I spent a lot of time in the steam room. I continued doing this until I was 30 years old.

There was a waitress who worked at The Lounge that I hooked up with a few times. I was not feeling it with her, so I passed her down to my boy, Stacy. Rest in peace. I saw him at The Lounge with his brother all the time. He took her for a spin and decided he wanted to *marry* her. After some time, they got *engaged*. Hey, I am not here to judge. It *worked* out so I was *happy* for him. She was not for me so I left her alone.

One night, as I was sitting in The Lounge, Royce walked in. He was one of my boys. We met through G. I knew him well. He walked in with his friend, Q, and a few women. We all got to laughing, playing pool and singing to the Chris Brown song *Deuces* off the juke box. Tina was one of the women they walked in with. She and I connected and vibed pretty well.

We all decided to *leave* The Lounge. They asked me if I wanted to roll and head to Q's house. We stopped to get a few Four Lokos alcoholic drinks, which had just *hit* the market and were beginning to gain *popularity* at the time. A few places eventually *banned* them because of the potential side effects.

When we got there, Q started to show me around the house. First, he decided to show me the massive orgy of at least ten people getting busy in his room. Mind you, these people were *already* at his house before we even got there. I could not believe what I was seeing. There were naked people everywhere. No one had any clothes on.

I enjoyed talking to Tina, so I did not partake in the escapade. Instead, she and I sat on the couch and talked until about 3:30 in the morning. At that point, I went home. I had a few hours to spare before I needed to get up and begin my day.

Such encounters were an *ongoing* thing at Q's house. One night when we were all together, I did participate. It was almost like being in a movie. It was emotionless, full of action, and people getting workouts you would not find at the gym. There were roughly 15 other people in that room, getting it on with each other. After sex swapping multiple women, I realized that lifestyle was not for me.

Whenever you walked into his house, you did not hear anything but the *immediate* conversation you were having. However, as you walked further down the hall and opened the bedroom door, all you could hear was moaning and the sound of sex leaving its *permanent* imprint on the walls, paint, floor, and bed.

Tina and I *continued* to talk for a while. I did *like* her and thought we were a *good* match. However, she had *three* kids from a previous long term relationship. I was not *looking* for a long term relationship, nor did I *want* one. I most certainly did not want to have a family of that size with her by any means. I was *content* with the sexual relationship we had going on and tried to keep it that way.

One day while we were on the phone, she started to talk about dating on a higher level. That day, I *stopped* the relationship and never spoke to her again. I had a one-track mind, and it did not involve a relationship, let alone one that would *add* three other kids to the mix.

The Lounge Bar & Grill was never short of *surprises* for who could and would walk through the door, as well as the things I could and would get myself. One evening, I saw this woman that I thought was cute. I liked the way she strutted around, walked around the bar, and did her thing with her homegirls.

We exchanged contact information.

After that night, we saw each other a *few* times around the bar before deciding to do anything or make any moves toward hanging out.

One night, after we started hanging out, her and her cousin came over after leaving the bar and grill. Her cousin was her roll buddy. They were *always* together. Her cousin stayed in my spare bedroom, and she stayed in my bed. I slept with her cousin first.

That next morning, her cousin went out for a morning McDonald's run. While her cousin was gone, I went back to my room and had sex with her. After her cousin returned, they *both* ended up in my bed. I had no clue if this was going to work, but I was definitely into pushing boundaries at the time. If they had gotten mad...oh well, they would have left and I would have moved on to the next. However, since they were cool with it, so was I.

That was my mentality.

Selfish.

Destructive.

That was my *justification* for living that way.

The 3 a.m. Catch Up

Being a massage therapist *requires* me to put my hands on people for a living. At any given time, I put my hands on people, anywhere from 60 minutes to two and a half hours per session. This kind of contact can allow a person's energy to *transfer* to you.

I did not *discriminate* who I would and would not put my hands on. I was there to *serve* every client and help *rid* their body of pain. I just wanted to *assist* everyone I met. I was also running loose through the streets, having sex like it was a sport. I was sleeping with women like it was going out of style.

At one point, in the middle of having sex with a lady, I started having this debate in my head.

"Jason you are gay."

"No, you are not!"

"Yes, you are."

"No, you are not!"

"Yes, you are. You had sexual interactions with another boy. You are gay!"

I had no clue what was *causing* these thoughts. *No clue.* These thoughts were giving me severe anxiety, and not to mention insecurity to the point I struggled to get an erection. I was afraid I would not get hard, therefore I was not and I did not feel like the man. My confidence was low. I was not in a comfortable place with myself.

This *internal* argument went on in my head for a few months. I had no clue what was going on and why these thoughts were taking place in my head. At my core, I knew I was not gay on any level. I still had no clue why these thoughts were *arresting* me at this point in my life. This awful ping-pong game, going back and forth in my mind, was *consuming* every aspect of my day.

As I was in the middle of having sex, these thoughts would show up and take all the fun out of it and ruin my flow. I had to face and deal with this just like I did that *unforgettable* day at the pool as an early adolescent, when I asked God to *erase* the memory of my childhood trauma.

A few times, I left the room after having sex to sit in the dark on the living room couch, telling myself that everything was going to be okay. After some time, I realized these thoughts had nothing to do with whether I was gay or not. Instead, I needed to deal with my *childhood* and the *past* correctly. It took me a little time to *understand* this and come to the revelation of what was happening.

I massaged gay men and lesbians as well. It did not matter. All I cared about was getting *every* client out of pain and helping *each* body function at its *highest* capacity. I have nothing *against* gay men or women by any means.

When I was working on them, I was evaluating their energy, but also taking it in unknowingly. The energy of every person I massaged was *attaching* itself to me, which was causing me to feel confused. However, I could no longer keep up with it. It was a sign to me that I needed to deal *appropriately* with my childhood.

God has a *weird* way of showing up. But when He does...*He does*. As an adult, my *perception* of life was not the same as when I was a child. What *affected* me as a child had a different *influence* on me as an adult. What you push to the *dark* will always come to light to *reveal* itself. That Friday afternoon, on a hot summer, as I sat in the kiddie pool, I asked God to take the pain *away* from me. Well, He did, so I could live my life and grow up to *become* a young man.

Now that I was an adult, the pain had to *resurface* to be properly dealt with. If I were in my *right* mind back then, emotionally and energetically, working on gay men and women would not have had the same effect that it did on me.

It was time!

At first, I did not quite know *how* to handle it.

I came across a fantastic therapist named Christy Belz. I met Christy at M.E. She was a client of mine, before I started seeing her. Her coming into my room that day for a massage was supposed to have been for *her*, but she was there to meet *me* and begin to *help* me. I will never forget the interaction we had and how the therapy session *benefited* me. I could not go back to see her because she was pretty expensive for my budget as a 23-year-old.

Our one session was a *catalyst* and *planted* seed for some *great* things to come and *grow* in my life. She planted a seed that would sprout in a way I did not think was possible. One of the most *profound* parts of our session was when she asked me to *travel* in my mind back to my childhood and *relive* certain events.

During this time, I picked out the moment I walked away from my friends at the baseball field and left them hitting balls without me. I remembered crying and weeping as I was walking home, full of the fear that I was *dying* from AIDS. My body was *shaking*. My heart was *racing* and felt like it was going to *rip* through my chest and *out* of my clothes. No place was *safe* for me emotionally that day or for most of that period of my life.

Christy instructed me to *transport* my adult self in my mind *back* in time, *meet* my young self, and *take* him to a safe place. I was to *hold* him in my arms, all the while telling him that everything was going to be *okay* and that I was *protected*.

When I went back in time to *protect* and save the younger Jason, I chose to take my younger self to my *sister's* room. That was a *safe* place. I cannot remember *why* I chose her room, but I did. Her room was all pink. I gained a lot of healing from this one visit, but I also knew that I had not scratched the surface of the work I *needed* to do and where this had to go.

It was a lot for me to do emotionally. I kept the ball rolling and was open to *uncovering* more of my past. This was a *massive* step in the *right* direction. I was able to see *clearer* than I had in a long, long time. I began to *see* the direction I needed to go.

A few days later, a *close* friend of mine reached out to me so he could spend some time in Denver. He had never been to Denver before and was looking for some fun. Since he could work *remotely*, all he needed was a computer and a place to *charge* his electronics. We made plans for him to touch down in a few weeks so we could have a great time *celebrating* my 24th birthday over the weekend.

I assured him that when he touched down, I would have something *special* waiting for him. When he arrived, we went back to my apartment so that he could *settle* in. About 30 minutes later, there was a knock on the door. I let the person into the apartment. It was a woman I knew who was going through a divorce.

I invited her to come over for my friend, who had never been to Denver before. I wanted the first thing he received as a warm welcome to be sex at the door. She obliged and she did her part well for my friend. I wanted to put on a show for him as he arrived in my city. I wanted him to go back home with some stories and always remember Denver. My friend stayed for a few weeks before returning home to New Jersey. We had a great time.

We had a few women come back to the apartment that we met while out and about, as we *maneuvered* through the streets of Denver. He was pretty comfortable with being in big cities by himself and figuring out the layout, so I *trusted* him with my Dodge Charger. He would drop me off at work so he could get a true sense of Denver on his own. He would pick me up from work and we would take the town by storm at night.

The high school years we had spent growing up with Cadillac Sam were great because we were no longer *afraid* of talking to women. "The worst thing they can say is no." The *worst* action they can give you is a *hostile* look before walking away, "Why you talking to me? You ugly."

I learned that women love when a man can make them *authentically* laugh or smile. I had developed the skill of picking up women as I drove by them in my car. Singing to them at the stoplight with my window down. Driving next to each other at the same velocity on the street. This was a natural ice breaker and *usually* successful.

As my friend and I drove around in my Charger, this was one of our strategies for getting women and having a good time. As far as memories are concerned, he and I made history together in Denver and a friendship for a lifetime.

To this day, we are still *great* friends.

We grandly celebrated my 24th birthday, definitely one for the record books. That particular night started slow, but it ended in a way I never thought possible. If I could describe it using any real frame of reference, it would have to be like the first *Hangover* movie.

My friend was *determined* to get bottle service for us that night; I was cool either way. I just wanted to have a *chill* night with a few drinks and good women surrounding me.

He replied, "Naw, forget that" with a demand and assurance that we were going to do this differently and put a *stamp* on it. "Your birthday night is going to be the best. We ain't settling for walk-in service, bro." Those were his words and pre-game pep talk to me. Bottle service at this club came with one bottle of Sky Vodka and two bottles of Champagne.

We *killed* the bottle of Sky Vodka, no problem. We made it through the first half of the first bottle of Champagne; then, it got *wild*. I *lost* my shirt and ended up on the *main* stage with an old school, crip gangster, who had a stunning woman with him that we wanted to meet. The *best* bottle service area was on the main stage.

While on the stage with him and his crew, I *threw* money in the air toward the crowd gathered around us. All the while, I thought I was throwing ones. Well, I did not realize until the next day that I had actually been throwing everything in the air *except* ones. I was throwing twenties and hundreds.

We started the night out with a grand and returned home with $400. The bottle service was $150. I lost everything else to the crowd! That was one hell of a night. No night of partying has *topped* that night.

To this day, we still *joke* about it.

After he left, things quickly went back to normal. We could have kept things going for another few weeks, but Denver needed us to chill for a while and take a break based on the road we were headed.

I still moved women through my apartment like there was no tomorrow. There was one single month where I had 40 women come through my apartment. One of them included one of the neighbors in my building. She was always walking past me smelling good. My brain and eyes said loudly, "I gotta give that a try before she moves out of here." That eventually happened, though I never saw her again.

I was so *preoccupied* with making conquests that I *overlooked* the destruction and pain I was *perpetuating*, simply because I was attempting to *fill* a void I did not want to address.

Early one morning around 3 a.m., as I was coming home from a night out of fun, I pulled out the key and stuck it in the brass colored door knob to *unlock* my apartment door. A Voice in my mind *resounded* before I could completely turn the key counter-clockwise to unlock the door, "After all this, you are still coming home alone!" It was *profound* and *loud*, yet a *quiet* moment in my life.

That voice was right. I was not *looking* for a wife or a girlfriend by any means. However, after all the sexcapades and *spending* money all night like I had it, I was still *empty* inside, attempting to *fill* the void in my life with sex and *meaningless* actions. All to *drown out* the reality that I needed to make a *change* and deal with Jason.

That was a profound occurrence in my life—a *defining incident*. For the *rest* of my life, I will never *forget* the Voice or what it *meant* to me.

Ponder over these words from King Solomon.

"My son, keep the rule of your father, and have in memory the teaching of your mother:

"Keep them ever folded in your heart, and have them hanging round your neck.

"In your walking, it will be your guide; when you are sleeping, it will keep watch over you; when you are awake, it will have talk with you.

"For the rule is a light, and the teaching a shining light; and the guiding words of training are the way of life.

"They will keep you from the evil woman, from the smooth tongue of the strange woman.

"Let not your heart's desire go after her fair body; let not her eyes take you prisoner.

"For a loose woman is looking for a cake of bread, but another man's wife goes after one's very life.

"May a man take fire to his breast without burning his clothing?

"Or may one go on lighted coals, and his feet not be burned?

"So it is with him who goes in to his neighbor's wife; he who has anything to do with her will not go free from punishment," (Proverbs 6:20-29).

The Sexual Shift

The realization from that early morning experience *punched* me in the back of the head. It took a *few* hours for my thoughts to wrap around what happened. I laid on the bed while God had a *conversation* with me.

"Jason, sit with yourself for a while. You have always filled the void of Me with sex and being around many others, never feeling comfortable with just being alone and at home. Just because you are by yourself does not mean you are alone."

I was laying on the bed looking at the TV. It was off, but the bathroom light was on. It was a *pleasant* yet *powerful* conversation. It brought me *comfort* and there was no *pressure* forcing me to change my ways. I *freely* knew the *time* for *change* had come.

That morning, I decided that no more women would come through the apartment for a nightcap or naked escapades on any level. I was not going to bring any woman *back* home from The Lounge. I decided to *stop* entertaining women sexually.

It happened so *naturally*.

I did not have to *fight* it or *resist* it.

It felt *amazing* to be in this place.

I started *reading* more and spending time by *myself.* I *still* went to The Lounge to play pool and have a great time. However, the narrative now was *different.*

My mindset was different.

I *saw* through a different *lens.*

I was there for a different *reason.*

At the *end* of the night, the *only* thing I left with was a To Go order of French fries. I would go home, pop in *Two and a Half Men* with Charlie Sheen, eat my fries and have a good laugh until I fell asleep.

Watching *Two and a Half Men* with Charlie was a *nightly* ritual for me. At the time, I could relate to Charlie on some level, which made it *twice* as hilarious for me *every* time I watched it. I had 60% of the series on DVD at the time. I would watch them over and over and laugh as though I had *never* seen the show before.

Sleeping on the couch became a *comfort* zone for me, just as it had been for me as a child. During this time, I *rarely* slept in my room. I typically *only* went into my room to get dressed or lie down for a while during the day. I *never* slept in that room at night, unless I had a woman come through, though that was on hold at this point.

As easy as my transition may seem, I was in an *uncomfortable* place as far as my energy was concerned. I had never moved like this before. I was *resisting* the temptation to have sex with the *first* woman that would *smile* at me. My apartment walls were not consumed with moaning noises or the movement of naked bodies filling space. I was no longer *depleting* my energy or *sabotaging* the visions I had for myself with unnecessary ejaculations that left all parties subconsciously confused about their own self-worth.

I was entering *new* territory.

A *new* Jason was surfacing, without really knowing the *outcome* of this transformation, while the *old* me was still trying to *keep* its presence known and nature going. Some nights were a *struggle*, so I occupied my time with other things. I spent more time *reading* books, *relaxing* in the steam room, and *watching* Two and a Half Men.

During this time, I became more *confident* because I saw myself in a new *light*; operating in a way my neurons, neuroplasticity, muscle twitches, and senses had not before. The old Jason was *losing* strength and momentum.

"What in the heck is going on here?" was a *constant* thought in my mind.

One morning, I was on the phone with my good friend, Candice. Candice was a childhood friend that I kept in touch with on a *regular* basis and still do to this day! She called me and I answered. I was picking out some clothes for the day. Out of the blue, as I was swiping through the clothes in my closet, trying to decide what to wear, I asked, Candice, "What happened to your friends that we went swimming with that day ten freaking years ago? Tatianna! How is she? Do you still talk to any of those girls from back then?"

I cannot recall her *entire* response, though she *still* kept in touch with her friend, Tai.

"Ahahahhaha," she responded giggling. "She's going through a not so pleasant divorce. Why did you bring her up?"

"I don't know. She just popped up in my head. I remember that one time we hung out at my dad's apartment pool that day and I am trying to have conversation with you."

"Yes she's going through a divorce. You should hit her up."

In my mind I was like, "Yo...we are only 25. What do you mean divorce? People get married at this time in their lives? Interesting...but ok."

I *found* her on Facebook and started *connecting* with her through direct messaging. We eventually linked up and saw each other in person. We had not seen each other in 10 or 11 years. It was crazy.

I will never forget *how* she walked into my apartment when we decided to meet up for the *first* time as *legal* adults. I told her I would *leave* the front door open. I was getting out of the shower and putting some jeans on. She came in *smiling*, with braids in her hair like she *owned* the place.

I was standing in my little hallway, tightening the belt to my Ralph Lauren jeans. I was wearing white Polo shoes, getting ready to take her to The Lounge Bar & Grill. It was not a formal date. We just wanted to catch up. Plus, I wanted to see how she responded to the environment I operated in.

We had a great time catching up. She stayed the *whole* night at my apartment and the crazy part is *nothing* happened. We just talked and laughed on my couch. After that night, my life was *never* the same.

Real Emotional Work Time

Tai and I dated for a while.

One night, as we were lying in bed with the lights off, I shared with her that in a few weeks I would be spending a week in Houston with my cousin and his wife. All I could make out was the silhouette of her sitting up in bed, *looking* in my direction. There was a street light facing my bedroom window *behind* her.

Her words *danced* in my ears, "I will take you."

From the way she said those four words, I knew I *loved* her and that she would be in my life for a while.

I had an *early* flight to Texas. It was at 4 a.m.

When I travel for fun, I like to get there *early* to hit the ground running and enjoy the *fullness* of the day there instead of *squandering* daylight traveling to my destination.

I had a *great* time in Houston, as I *always* do.

Tai and I dated for four years *before* we got married. I had a huge *emotional* challenge leading up to our marriage. I did not understand why everything was happening the way it did.

Towards the beginning of our dating years, a friend and I sparred with our words, checking in with each other about the *growth* we had been having in our own lives. Our birthdays fall on the same day, and we relate magnificently, so we liked to *challenge* each other.

She *interrogated*, "What do you like most about Tai and how are things going?"

I replied, "When we disagree, I do not feel the need to cheat on her or have sex with a random person." This used to be a way of life for me. That was important to me on a *grand* scale. It signaled to me that I was *beginning* to have a conscience, to *reawaken* the one within. Being hard and cold is a much easier habit to develop than having a *loving* and *open* heart.

The latter takes work...*consistent daily work.*

When I decided to cut off every woman in my phone, something would always pop up in my life that I refer to as *residue*. When you fire a gun, a residue *lingers* on your hands and clothes, depending on the type of weapon. When you open a can or package containing a powdery substance, some of it can get on you, whether a lot or a little.

This is precisely what I was facing. I got rid of all the women I had been talking to, yet I still had *their residue* on me. Given the sexual connection I had with all of them and the sexual energy I had been putting into the atmosphere for years, some things that I had been trying to let go of were still *attached* to me.

This put a lot of *strain* on the trust in my relationship with Tai. In 2013, I decided to *seek* counseling for sexual addiction. It was of my own volition and in the spur of the moment. The time had come for me to confront this and call it for what it was. A while back, Tai introduced me to Pastor K from the local church she was attending, so I decided to go give her a try. Plus, the cost of the sessions was in my budget at the time.

Going through the single counseling session with Christy, several years prior, was the *catalyst*. I was *open* to what would come out of meeting with Pastor K because of my *great* experience with Christy as well as my willingness to not resist what I was needing to face.

So often, men get turned away from seeking the proper help they need. They think they can solve the issues on their own or will not even admit they could use the help. Not resisting or pushing back on this kind of help is important for you as a man to recognize and use to your advantage. Most issues we face, we should not try or aim to solve on our own. When we try to fix our issues by ourselves, we end up making things worse or not getting to the root cause of certain things. It is like trying to self-diagnose.

To become emotionally healthy, I had to *keep* the ball rolling. Pastor K and I headed down the same path I did with Christy. Since my counseling session was provided through the church, it cost me only $25 per visit instead of $130.

I made some *significant* headway in my sessions with Pastor K, and then I *hit* a brick wall. It has been said, "Do not get distracted by the shiny things or shiny balls." That statement is *typically* made in a materialist sense or when you are dealing with a playful cat. It is *rarely* applied to interpersonal relationships.

Tai and I were going through a *rough* patch. I was fed up. I felt I was being taken advantage of and was *unappreciated*. Those were my feelings, not what was actually happening. As human beings, we are prone to making up *false* realities in our minds about what we *think* is happening versus what is *actually* happening. Therefore, we get to play victim.

During my stint as a steam room user, I would always run into *great* people, *exciting* people, *confused* people, and *quiet* people.

One day, I stopped at a store to get a pack of razors on my way to the steam room. I saw a woman whom I had spoken to a few times at the gym. We exchanged a few words. "Weird seeing you here. How are you?" I gave her my business card and moved along. A few moments later, I received a text.

"Great to see you J!"

This small exchange opened the door for a relationship over a period of time that was practically *emotional* cheating on Tai. It caused an *uproar*, intensifying the *tension* and *mistrust* that plagued our relationship.

Here is a perfect example of how things are not always what they seem. That shiny ball may not be all that shiny. There was *nothing* shiny about this other individual and I am thankful I saw that *early* on.

At this moment in time, I learned never to allow my spirit, mind and heart to be *open* to recklessness again. We often permissively *allow* things to enter our lives that we have *more* control over than we give ourselves credit.

If we become more *mindful* of our situations, of what we do and *permit* into our lives, we would have a *higher* success rate in *dealing* with the drama, *surviving* mistrust, *healing* emotional brokenness, and *picking up* the pieces of the messes we made.

After I *assessed* everything that had transpired, I *removed* that individual from my life and shared what had happened with Tai. I discovered I was now *stronger* on many playing fields because I now knew what *shiny* distractions looked like and how *opposing* forces can try to meet you with the same amount of resistance that you put out. This was an *empowering* revelation, a game-changer, and *strengthened* my toolbelt of awareness when *handling* situations with the opposite sex.

As I continued the counseling sessions with Pastor K, this time proved extremely valuable. They made me *aware* of what was going on through a *different* lens. I am thankful I hung in there and continued to *resist* the opposing force, that was wanting me to stay right where I was, with a *greater* amount of force engaged for a *longer* period of time. The opposing force had no choice but to surrender.

I was making *fewer* mistakes. I could *easily* have made some choices that would have led to the *demise* of our relationship. I would have run my relationship with Tai into oblivion, *ruining* just about everything good that I had going on in my life at the time.

I was *thankful* for Pastor K's presence in my life.

Her sensitivity, wisdom, her ability to relate and not give up on me.

Since I did not have sex with the woman from the gym, it made it so much easier to *build* a stronger relationship with Tai and to be able to tell her the *entire* truth about everything.

I did not have to fight or *hide* guilt.

My conscience was *clear*.

My moral compass was *stronger*.

Before making my counseling commitment with Pastor K, I felt it was important for Tai to *know* the number of women I had taken to bed. I had no *shame* in my game, and this level of *transparency* was *vital* for me. When I *shared* that information with her, it was not because she *forced* it. It did not come up in a *heated* conversation, nor was it *her* idea.

I *wanted* her to know.

There had been *over* 150 women I had slept with over the course of my life up to this point in time. I was 26 years old. Sharing this information with her benefited our relationship in a *significant* way.

I wanted her to know.

A lot of couples *avoid* and neglect this subject. I feel it is extremely important to have this level of *openness*. Some couples act like they do not need to know, or want to know. It is vital to be this open and transparent regardless of the number. You have to communicate here. It is not about the number, but rather the *trust*. We have been able to *joke* about it at times as we were out in public.

If I say, "She looks familiar from somewhere."

She replies, "Oh, did you sleep with her too?"

It took some time to bounce back from the steam room girl situation and get the air *cleared*. Honestly, I am *thankful* it happened. There may have been some emotional distress during the process; however, I *learned* about myself and how the enemy can *attempt* to use your past weaknesses to *derail* your future and *lead* you right back into your *old* ways.

Once again, the words of King Solomon ring so true. "My son, give attention to my wisdom; let your ear be turned to my teaching:

"So that you may be ruled by a wise purpose, and your lips may keep knowledge.

"For honey is dropping from the lips of the strange woman, and her mouth is smoother than oil;

"But her end is bitter as wormwood, and sharp as a two-edged sword;

"Her feet go down to death, and her steps to the underworld;

"She never keeps her mind on the road of life; her ways are uncertain, she has no knowledge.

"Give ear to me then, my sons, and do not put away my words from you.

"Go far away from her, do not come near the door of her house;

"For fear that you may give your honour to others, and your wealth to strange men:

"And strange men may be full of your wealth, and the fruit of your work go to the house of others;

"And you will be full of grief at the end of your life, when your flesh and your body are wasted;

"And you will say, How was teaching hated by me, and my heart put no value on training;

"I did not give attention to the voice of my teachers, my ear was not turned to those who were guiding me!

"Let water from your store and not that of others be your drink, and running water from your fountain.

"Let not your springs be flowing in the streets, or your streams of water in the open places.

"Let them be for yourself only, not for other men with you.

"Let blessing be on your fountain; have joy in the wife of your early years.

"As a loving hind and a gentle doe, let her breasts ever give you rapture; let your passion at all times be moved by her love.

"Why let yourself, my son, go out of the way with a strange woman, and take another woman in your arms?

"For a man's ways are before the eyes of the Lord, and he puts all his goings in the scales.

"The evil-doer will be taken in the net of his crimes, and prisoned in the cords of his sin.

"He will come to his end for need of teaching; he is so foolish that he will go wandering from the right way," (Proverbs 5:15-23).

My sessions with Pastor K lasted six months.

From October of 2013 to April of 2014. That was the *push* I needed. My relationship with Tai got back on track. After some time had passed, I knew it was *time* to get baptized.

In May of 2014, I did just that. This was the *final* piece to the puzzle for me. I did not expect this to happen. I was not looking for it. I just did not resist when the revelation came to me.

If God revealed to you the entire destination and the things you would endure along the way, you would give up before you even started. That is why we are not shown the whole path or journey all at once or at the beginning.

Getting Baptized

Before this, I never had any *interest* in baptism.

However, *after* my sessions with Pastor K, I decided to take the Baptism Class. I had no real clue what was in store for me, but I was darn sure I would not *resist* this opportunity to grow.

The Baptism Class was a four-week, 90 minutes a week course. The ten other men in the class were on a similar, but *unique* journey to Baptism, including a nine-year-old boy. I was not there to *judge* anyone else's journey, though I was *proud* to see the youngin' taking this *big* step. I was happy seeing him *gaining* this knowledge, *improving* his self-control, and getting *closer* to the Lord. At nine, I was thinking about magic fries and playing basketball, not getting baptized.

Hearing the powerful stories of the other men was very *impactful*. I even got a little teary-eyed, as did some of the other men there. I *enjoyed* getting to know them and *hearing* their stories. One word cannot describe what I learned in that class, but rather a phrase or an analogy. I realized the importance and value of *removing* *all* of the emotional sex ties I had with the women I previously had in my life. I was not *broken*; however, I was not spiritually and emotionally *whole* either.

If you take a *piece* of swiss cheese, it may be a *perfect* square; however, there are *holes* in it. The holes represent your *weak* areas in life that need patching, or better yet, *filling* with love and the *removal* of unworthiness.

This was a game-changer.

I knew from that moment on how the enemy had been *derailing* me, *using* me, *weakening* me, and making it *harder* for me to be the *highest* version of myself possible. He was *stopping* me from reaching my goals, let alone having a *healthy* relationship.

Constantly revisiting my past nature, through such physical actions, would unconsciously *strip* me of the *healthy* bond I was developing with who I was becoming. It would even put me on a journey that would *negatively* affect my son, both emotionally and spiritually. I would be *perpetuating* a generational cycle of *emptiness* and *destruction*, that he would then *harness, spew out,* and then *pass down.* That class had more in store for me than I could have ever imagined.

Your journey through Baptism may be different, or maybe it already was. Shoot, or maybe you have not got baptized at all. I developed a *clear* understanding of how the enemy was *destroying* my greatness and self-worth; through my past and only my past. I allowed the *wrong* seeds to get attached to me for *corrupt* germination, therefore sprouting into a tree bearing *bad* fruit.

Everything from that situation with Jeremy to my father had *framed* my past. I decided that the enemy will never use *myself* against me again in that manner. Never again will I *allow* the enemy to project my father's or mother's past or my upbringing as a *limitation* on my life. I may have inherited some spiritual baggage from my father, but it was up to me to *break* the cycle.

Daily, I *carry* with me the understanding and awareness of *where* I have been. The reality is, I can become cocky, overconfident, or *misuse* the tools with which I have been spiritually and emotionally equipped with. If I do so, I *risk* falling right back into the same pit from which I had to *grind* and *claw* my way out of. There is no crawling on an *uphill* climb.

The day of my Baptism was like the *sealing* of an envelope. I was *proud* of myself regardless of what anyone else had to say because I had *overcome* something *huge* in my life. Tai wanted to *invite* the whole world to *support* me. I did not want anyone there because this was *my* journey, and I could not do it for anyone *other* than myself. The people in my life were *beneficiaries* of what I had overcome and the chains that had been *broken*.

I will never forget that moment in time and what I *gained* from it. It was a *reward* and an investment that *keeps* on giving. It is much easier to *maintain* a garden by plucking weeds *daily*. I have had *plenty* of opportunities to pick up the habits from my past and cause destruction once again, *trading* the grand plan God has designed in exchange for a *temporary* thrill.

The *temptation* is there.

"Ooowww, Jason, you know you want to tap that and take it for a spin around the block."

"Maan, you could knock the dirt off homegirl and get right back to life."

"Look how she is looking at you. No one is around. You are in a different part of town where nobody knows you. Go hit that."

These are all conversations I have had with myself, and I am sure that *many* men have had these same thoughts. No one benefits or gains anything worth mentioning.

"Oh, he lasted long."

"Damn, I was stroking nice. That was awesome."

That high *fades* even before you finish getting the sentence out. By recognizing my weakness with sex, I was able to *reposition* it forever from being the *focal* point of my life. The awakening of this revelation made me aware that I was no longer *lame* or *weak*.

Instead, I am more *robust* in every way.

"You have been put to no test but such as is common to man: and God is true, Who will not let any test come on you which you are not able to undergo; but He will make with the test a way out of it, so that you may be able to go through it," (1 Corinthians 10:13).

One evening, I pulled up to a client's house while it was raining and snowing. I arrived *early*, so I had some time to kill. I called my mom because I wanted to fill her in on this feeling I was having about relationships and marriage before I started my massage session. I wanted to *process* my thoughts and *exchange* with my mom during this brief moment.

Prior to this period in my life, I had never been *concerned* with marriage or gave it much thought. The idea of it sounded *nice* but not much else. I was *content* with staying single. Nevertheless, I could *barely* keep it together as I talked to her.

I was *weeping* like a baby. I had never known this feeling or awakening about marriage before, or how it could look or feel. I could not go into detail with her over the phone because she was out to dinner with some friends. I simply told her there was something *important* I wanted to share with her.

After getting off the phone, I kept crying for another 30 seconds or so before I had to get my act together, gather my things and step out into the cold, so I could walk into my client's house.

A few days later, I went to my mom's house. I began to share what I had been feeling and where I was with Tai at this point in my life. I wanted to *marry* her. Once again, I was in tears. Not because of marriage itself, but rather how it felt to *open* my heart and not live *guarded* or *emotionless*. I felt more *whole* emotionally and spiritually at this very second than I ever had in my life. The flood gates had opened up. I had never felt this overwhelming emotion around Love. The key was I did not resist the feelings I was having or act like it was not real.

I was confident I had *overcome* some serious challenges related to women, the role they had previously played in my life, and how I perceived them now. This was an *uncomfortable* conversation for my mother because she was *losing* her son emotionally to *another* woman, based on the type of relationship the two of us had developed as I was growing up.

My mom and I had always been very *close*. Up until now, there had never been *another* woman who was a *stronger* candidate for my *time*, or person I would prefer to *lean on* in hard times, over her.

She was even taken *aback* by the growth I was experiencing and how it was *affecting* me at that very moment. I was in tears and needed tissue the whole time. I was just so *overcome* by sentiment, with the realization of what had been emotionally *stored up* for years. I could not hold it in.

Not too long after that conversation, Tai and I discussed marriage counseling. She was game, but only *after* we got engaged. I could see why she felt that way. However, I was on a slightly different trajectory as far as this decision and vision for our life was concerned.

I pointed out, "You have been married before, and it did not go well. I have never been married at all or even thought I would be. It has been said that the second marriage is more likely to fail than the first one." We were in quite a situation, I must say.

"We need to go to counseling and see if this is something we even want to pursue together or at all. If it is, then we can move forward. If we want the relationship to win, then we need to check this out first."

She was all *in* after I gave my perspective and view of our life together. She appreciated my leadership and ability to care for not just her, but the relationship. By taking an interest in the success of our marriage, I was *properly* caring for her.

We enrolled in a 12-week *Marriage 101* course through our church. Twelve other couples went through it with us. The *biggest* takeaways I gathered were that a husband and wife have *roles* they play in the marriage.

I am not referring to the "do not step out of line, you know your place" mentality. It has to do with *knowing* the strengths and weaknesses of each other and *recognizing* each person's capabilities so each person can fully step into that.

For example, within our home, I am not that strong when it comes to *disciplinary* actions. I do not recognize the moments discipline has to be dispensed as well as my wife does. I am more of a *talker*, "Hey, let us talk this out. Sit yo' behind down and let us find out what is going on."

I handle conflict in *public* better than she does, so I usually take the *lead* in those situations. She is better at calling to *settle* bills or getting vendors to the house for maintenance. Since I meet with clients for most of the day and evening, she can cover those areas on the home front.

We have an *ongoing* understanding of who handles what, and sometimes these shift around. The key here is ego is removed and there is no resisting. Sometimes it is important for me to step in to lighten her load a little.

In the class, we learned that ego should not *hinder* what has to be done, so we *remove* our egos to the best of our ability. It can be *challenging* at times, do not get it twisted, we are human *beings* not doings. Set your *pride* and *egos* aside so the relationship can *win* and not an individual party.

This was a *big* takeaway for us, even though we did not *realize* it at the time. I sincerely *wish* the class could have lasted *longer*, because within 12 weeks, at 90 minutes a pop, you have not even begun to scratch the surface of some issues or traumas.

Tai and I are *grateful* to have taken the class and for the other couples that were a part of it.

No Longer On The Market

In the summer of 2015, we decided to take a cruise with our kids and extended family. I had never been on one before, but Tai had, and she wanted us to experience it *together*. I figured this would be an *excellent* time to ask her to be my wife.

Before this, I had to come up with *how* and *where* I would propose. I am not super creative, but I had a few ways to make this a success. I *needed* her dad's blessing. It took a while, but I *eventually* got it.

It was not a *simple* conversation, "May I have your daughter's hand in marriage?" followed by an *immediate*, "Why, yes, son. You have my blessing."

We had a *long* conversation where I explained my *vision* for what our marriage would look like and accomplish. At the end of it, he answered, "Thanks, son. I will think about it and get back to you."

It took an *additional* four days for him to get back to me. I do not think he *wanted* me to marry his daughter, considering I was "scrubadub" before I met her. I do not *blame* him. He was not going to make it *easy* either, so I *respect* that.

No father wants anything *wrong* to happen to any of his children, especially to his daughter within the *commitment* of a marriage relationship. It is not a *light* matter to give your daughter to another man, especially if she has been *heartbroken* before. His blessing meant a lot to me. I was *thankful* for his acceptance.

On the last night of the cruise, I asked Tai to marry me. We had gathered toward the *back* of the cruise ship. The kids were with us. I told her to close her eyes. I put on a shirt written, "Will you marry me?"

I had hoped that we would run into her parents so they could be a part of it; however, everything happened the way it was supposed to.

The Lord Jesus spoke about marriage.

"For this cause will a man go away from his father and mother, and be joined to his wife;

"And the two will become one flesh; so that they are no longer two, but one flesh.

"Let not that which has been joined together by God be parted by man," (Mark 10:7-9).

After we got married, I still had a lot of growing up to do. I needed to *understand* what it meant to be a husband and be in the husband's position. There were boundaries I still did not understand, not for my sake, but my wife's.

A wife wants to *know* and *feel* she is number *one* in her husband's life. Period. I thought I had made that apparent, but I was at a loss about what that meant from an *active* position. It was great for her to tell me what she needed. However, I was still not getting it.

I was *confident* and believed that just because I was not cheating or sleeping around, and we were now married, I was doing things *right*. I presumed I was off to a *great* start. Only after you put your wife or significant other *first* can they experience *freedom* in a way they can feel it to their *core*.

The Apostle Paul wrote, "Husbands, have love for your wives, even as Christ had love for the church, and gave Himself for it," (Ephesians 5:25).

I always enjoy *meeting* new people, taking them to *lunch* to get to know them, and learning how I can *serve* them (my clients) better.

Both men and women.

I enjoy *connecting* with people.

Well, if I am doing all this with *other* people and *neglecting* to take my wife out to lunch or on dates, she is *eventually* going to feel a type of way about that.

My wife got *upset* with me over this. I did not understand what she meant. Over time it *clicked* for me. It took some hard work and removing my ego to *accept* what my wife was requesting and needing. I had to make her know she is number *one* in a way *she* would *understand* it.

I am thankful for the *revelation* and the *ability* to make the changes I *needed* to be a married man. I was still *early* in the development of my maturity in relationships. I still needed fine-tuning so I could be fully present on the path I was walking. I had a *substantial* mental transition to make, moving from a boy to a man.

Healing Through My Father

In May of 2015, my father was diagnosed with early-onset dementia. When he called to let me know, the *reality* of it had not sunk in yet. He was not upset or angry. Only *slightly* sad and probably a *little* scared.

I wanted to understand *why* he got it and why this was the way his story was going to *end*. I asked God for *clarity* and eventually received *all* the answers I needed, although they did not all come through at once.

I was on a run outside one day after he had shared his situation with me. I just lost it. I cried like a baby and had to *stop* in the middle of my run to let it all out before I could continue. I went back into counseling, but this time with the man that performed our marriage ceremony, Pastor JC. He is one of the *greatest* men I have ever known and confided in.

Together, we went down a *long* journey of emotional healing in a way that *revealed* to me that I had no clue how *deep-rooted* the challenges were that had been *slowing* me down and the *core* causes of the destruction I had experienced in my life.

I did not realize, nor was I aware of, how *angry* I was with my father as I was growing up. I *loved* my dad. He did the *best* he could. Yet, I was *hurt* more by *him* than I was by my mom. This blew my mind to the point I cried at the drop of a dime just *thinking* about it all. It also meant I still had a lot to work out and through.

I presumed my issues revolved around my mom.

I was way off.

When I discovered this, I was an emotional wreck. I had *stuffed* this all down on the inside of me for the *longest* time. I did not realize the impact it was having on me. Now that I had clarity, I knew I could get more *resilient*, emotionally and spiritually. I could get on a trajectory that would lead me into my *greatness* as a man, a husband, a father, a son of God, and a businessman.

In September of 2018, Pastor told me that I needed to make things *right* with my dad *before* he passed away. I had to share *why* I loved him, *what* I loved about him, why I was *angry* with him, and that I was *sorry* for the wrong things I did in our relationship.

I thought this was a *pointless* act. "I can just say it to myself and have the same impact, right?"

Wrong! (He was still alive.)

"Jason, your dad may have dementia, but you have no clue what he can and cannot understand."

"Well, Pastor, you have a point there I must say." Just because my dad could not *speak*, that did not mean he could not *understand* the words I was *feeding* him. Several months earlier, I could not have gone through with this because I knew that I would *cry* in front of my dad. I mean straight lose it. I did not want him to think or feel that he was *dying* right then and there, plus I did not want him to *see* me crying from my core in sadness. I had *avoided* it like Bruce Lee dodging punches and kicks.

I *looked* him in his face, *held* his hand with confidence, and shared with him *everything* that I was feeling and what I talked about in counseling. I did not *cry*, nor did I *hold* anything back. I had just begun to understand this whole thing differently, so it *hit* me in a new light. This cathartic experience was no longer for him, *but me!*

I walked out a *new* person from the rehabilitation facility where my dad was temporarily staying. I had *shed* my old skin. The healing I received that day began to *impact* my marriage in a new way...*a marvelous way*.

Have you ever *craved* something in your life so *severely*, and when you *got* it, you did not know what to do with it? That is what was happening with my wife. She had been praying for me and had not seen the *manifestation* of it yet.

When she started noticing that my actions and views had *changed* and reflected what she had been *asking* God to do in my life, she did not know how to react. She *rejected* some of it as if it was not real. I even appeared to be *fake* to her because she had not seen any of it before.

I was beginning to operate in a new way, moving in a more *powerful* posture in every aspect of my life.

Whenever you make *changes*, you will be faced with an *equal* force of *resistance*. There were moments when the *old* habits would *attempt* to make a *guest* appearance. I would *recognize* them, regroup, and move forward. I continued to experience this ebb and flow until the old habits no longer made any more appearances.

Shortly after my emotional experience with my father, he was sent home to be taken care of for the *remainder* of his life in hospice care; by his wife, my sister, three other caretakers and myself. I made arrangements with his wife to stay overnight *twice* a week and watch over him so she could *rest*. This allowed me to spend time with him.

There was *never* a two-way communication ordeal. I changed his clothes, moved him around, and tucked him in bed. Whenever he would look at me, he *knew* who I was. He had this look that he had never seen me before, yet he knew *who* I was. He looked surprised, yet *glad* to see me.

It was like meeting one of your close friends on the street you have not seen in a while. You run up to them and shake hands with the authority and the strength that real *recognizes* real. There is a *bond* between the two of you. That handshake represents every *interaction* you two have had.

That is how it was *every* time I saw my dad.

On Friday, May 3rd, 2020, at 1:30 a.m., my father passed on. That night I had been *struggling* to fall asleep, so I completely missed the call. It was one of those nights you cannot fall asleep, yet you know that morning is *creeping* up on you to *slap* you in the face so you can wake your butt up. You avoid looking at the clock to prevent the *disappointment* of how much time you have left before you have to get out of bed.

When I looked at my phone, I checked my voicemail and it was the voice of my uncle announcing my father had passed. I hopped out of bed and went over to keep his wife company, as we waited for the coroner to pick up his body.

When I got to his house, I walked in and saw his still *lifeless* body. I began to *clap* my hands in praise and thanksgiving because I was so *grateful* he passed at home and for the amount of time I spent with him. I was able to make everything right *before* his departure. I *hugged* him one last time, *kissed* him, and I *closed* his eyes. I could not have been more thankful than at that moment.

After the coroner picked up his body, I went to *work*. Yes, I *went* to work. I closed my man's eyes then went to *serve* my clients. Taking the day off to *sulk* and *cry* would not *help* me or do me any *good*. I had *eight* sessions on the docket for the day and could not let those people *down*. That also would have taken *away* from my household.

My dad was *gone* now, but I had to *keep* going.

If it was not for the *intense* work I did at counseling, and in the *privacy* of my own home, I would not have been able to *keep going* as I did. I will write his name a few times to keep it relevant:

Judson H. Thompson

Judson H. Thompson

Judson H. Thompson from the Bronx.

Thank you. I am grateful to you in every possible way. I gained some huge wins through this healing journey from which my family will *continue* to reap the *benefits* for generations to come. I *severed* any *destructive* chains from the generations that went *before* me. I *cancel* them off my family and off the people *beyond* my life's grasp, who will be *impacted* by my life and decisions.

The Outcome

I developed a *healthier*, more *impactful* outlook on my life through my healing journey. I gained an *understanding* of my molestation and its *impact*, the healing I needed, along with the manifestations of it over the course of my life, the *habits* I picked up from my father, and the *healing* I needed related to him.

I have a more *hopeful* outlook on life, with a higher chance of being my *true* self. I do not *regret* what happened to me as a kid. The impact and ripple effect were astronomical *beyond* measure. I had to go through a lot of healing. I do not *blame* Jeremy for what he did. The reality and truth is, someone was doing it to him *first*. Understanding this takes away all of the power from Jeremy and the situation.

Many days I *looked* in the mirror and *faced* the things I did not necessarily want to address. I have dug *deep* just to make right what was wrong in my life. I took the time to *understand* all aspects of my destructive lifestyle and its root *causes*. I *endured* counseling to take the sting away so it can never have that death grip on me again.

I spent a lot of time and emotional energy, making myself *whole* again. It has been one hell of a ride, but it has been *worth* it. The profits from this investment pay off over and over again. I have *broken* the cycle of destruction in my family and among my three boys and daughter.

I can deliver a *healthier* line of communication and *guide* them without *baggage* or a *broken* spirit, as well as prevent some of it from happening to them as well. I live *without* selfishness, and emotional or spiritual attachments from the past, that many carry. My wife gets a *complete* version of myself and a *healthier*, more *authentic* level of love from me.

With all of the trauma I had endured and collected in my younger years, the only thing I was good for was making *whole* people broken, and if they were broken, I helped *break them down even more* and make them feel *less* worthy.

When my children come to me for advice or just want to share something with me, they receive *wisdom* and not a personal narrative of daggers, shields, and tools of destruction. They receive *agape love* in return. They see and experience *love*, so they have a stronger understanding of *how* to deliver it.

The *rewards* of being a healed, loving man *outweigh* the results of sleeping with every woman I come across and only thinking about how the interactions will benefit *me*. What I thought was helping me was delivering *negatives* and *losses* in my life. What you do to another can have *massive* repercussions you may or may not have intended.

"Be not tricked; God is not made sport of: for whatever seed a man puts in, that will he get back as grain.

"Because he who puts in the seed of the flesh will of the flesh get the reward of death; but he who puts in the seed of the Spirit will of the Spirit get the reward of eternal life.

"And let us not get tired of well-doing; for at the right time we will get in the grain, if we do not give way to weariness," (Galatians 6:7-9).

Lessons, Oh The Lessons We Learn

Throughout this book, I shared many of the lessons I learned that have helped me *evolve* and *grow* into the man I am today.

Extract the lessons that are contained in these stories so that you can *avoid* leaving a trail of destruction in your wake. Choose to live like a *real* man and not as a boy. As a man, you will face many opportunities that will be *defining* moments for you, if you will set your dial to them after they happen or while they are happening.

They will serve as a *beacon* for your intuition.

They will help you *understand* the lessons you need to learn, and the right *direction* you are supposed to go. Many times we put ourselves in situations that do not benefit us in any possible way. These become *significant* setbacks, *prolong* our progress, and *delay* us from reaching our goals and potential.

If we take a little more time to work through scenarios in *advance*, we can save ourselves from a lot of *trouble* and *wasted* time. The stories I shared reveal how each of those situations are more *detrimental* than good, and more *harmful* than beneficial. I was truly operating in a place of lack and not abundance.

The *deeper* you get, the *longer* and more *intense* your *recovery* time becomes. The *further* you move away from being the man you are meant to be, the more *drastic* and *painful* your recovery will have to be.

Points To Remember

In parting, hold on to these truths.

Just because you are 18, 21, 25, 30, 40, or even 50 years old, does not *make* you a MAN. Your age does not *determine* if you are a man.

Know your worth.

Sit down and evaluate yourself. Do not just say you are worthy. *Know what that means to you.*

Ask yourself what destruction looks like for *you*? How does destroying someone *else* look?

Having a Penis does not entitle you to use it as a weapon. It should *serve* you. It is not for you to surrender to it.

Having sex with a large number of women does not empower you. It *weakens* you spiritually, emotionally, and *derails* you, leaving you feeling *empty* and *lacking* wholeness.

Having sex with a lot of women can leave you feeling very *confused* about who you are.

Sexually abusing someone else can leave them *scarred* in ways you cannot even imagine, especially if they are kids. If you think it might sound cool, think again.

Breathe *life* into others.

The more women you have sex with, the more energy you *deplete* and *waste*.

Before you have sex with her, ask yourself if she is a woman you will want to bring before your momma? Even if you do not have a mom, ask yourself the question. Could you proudly *introduce* her to your *loved* ones and those whose opinions you *value*?

If you feel the slightest *unease* about entering a sexual situation with another female, *listen* to instinct and find a *diversion*.

If you were *molested*, know you are still a human being, and that act does not *define* you. It may *haunt* you if you do not *face* and adequately *deal* with it.

Mental health is *essential*. Do not neglect it or think that it is only for women. Women are not the only species with a brain, feelings, or emotions.

Get your mind right through counseling. The *purpose* of counseling is to help you become the *highest* and *greatest* version of yourself. Do not try to *control* the counseling sessions and the outcome.

Know you are *worthy* of valuable relationships with great people and the *one* woman who wants to give you the world. *Yes, she is out there!*

King Solomon said, "Whoever gets a wife gets a good thing, and has the approval of the Lord," (Proverbs 18:22).

The energy you put *out* is the energy you get in *return*. I do not care about what aspect of life you are referring to.

Check your energy.

Ask yourself where you are *directing* your energy? Make a list of the areas in your life and ask yourself if you are giving those areas *too* much energy, or *not enough*, or whether or not you should even give them any at all?

If you are living an *unhealthy* sexual pattern and you want to break it, *you can*. Know you can and you *should*. Your flesh is not going to be happy with you, which is perfectly ok! You might experience some *resistance* through your *environment*, previous daily *habits*, and nostalgic *aromas* you may encounter.

"Let married life be honored among all of you and not made unclean; for men untrue in married life will be judged by God," (Hebrews 13:4).

Just because you are broken spiritually, you do not have to *stay* that way. I trust this book will be an *addition* to your life. Based on the insights in this book, may you become whole.

This transformation was absolutely *beautiful* to me and I am *thankful* it happened. I am always on a quest to *better* myself and the people *around* me. To this day I am in counseling on a *regular* basis. I feel and believe it is extremely *important* to *maintain* a healthy relationship with *yourself*, and one of those ways is through counseling.

We are *always* going to go through situations as life goes on and throws us curve balls from time to time. I *embrace* my family and the *value* they bring to my life. When I think about how awesome they are, it *excites* me and makes me want to keep *improving* for them.

Leading an *honest and disciplined* life allows you to be even more *free* than ever before. At one point I would have begged to differ. I would have said being reckless was a *better* option. You have more *freedom* on *this* side of the track.

The Apostle Paul documented, "Being certain of this, that no man who gives way to the passions of the flesh, no unclean person, or one who has desire for the property of others, or who gives worship to images, has any heritage in the kingdom of Christ and God," (Ephesians 5:5).

My relationship with the Lord has never been so strong or consistent. I *enjoy* spending time with

Him on a *daily* basis, *listening* to His instructions, and being *comforted* by His words and consistency. There is nothing like it. Thank You, Holy Spirit!

The Apostle Paul wrote these words of encouragement. "But I say, Go on in the Spirit, and you will not come under the rule of the evil desires of the flesh.

"For the flesh has desires against the Spirit, and the Spirit against the flesh; because these are opposite the one to the other; so that you may not do the things which you have a mind to do.

"But if you are guided by the Spirit, you are not under the law.

"Now the works of the flesh are clear, which are these: evil desire, unclean things, wrong use of the senses,

"But the fruit of the Spirit is love, joy, peace, a quiet mind, kind acts, well-doing, faith,

"Gentle behaviour, control over desires: against such there is no law.

"And those who are Christ's have put to death on the cross the flesh with its passions and its evil desires.

"If we are living by the Spirit, by the Spirit let us be guided.

"Let us not be full of self-glory, making one another angry, having envy of one another," (Galatians 5:16-19,22-26).

My relationship with the Lord has brought more *peace* to my home and family. Being in this space and having this mentality has kept me *out* of harm's way. This way of living has *protected* me from losing myself, my family and my career.

I am incredibly thankful.

"I am free to do all things; but not all things are wise. I am free to do all things; but I will not let myself come under the power of any.

"Food is for the stomach and the stomach for food, and God will put an end to them together. But the body is not for the desires of the flesh, but for the Lord; and the Lord for the body:

"And God who made the Lord Jesus come back from the dead will do the same for us by His power.

"Do you not see that your bodies are part of the body of Christ? how then may I take what is a part of the body of Christ and make it a part of the body of a loose woman? such a thing may not be.

"Or do you not see that he who is joined to a loose woman is one body with her? for God has said, The two of them will become one flesh.

"But he who is united to the Lord is one spirit.

"Keep away from the desires of the flesh. Every sin which a man does is outside of the body; but he who goes after the desires of the flesh does evil to his body.

"Or are you not conscious that your body is a house for the Holy Spirit which is in you, and which has been given to you by God? and you are not the owners of yourselves;

"For a payment has been made for you: let God be honored in your body," (1 Corinthians 6:12-20).

I do not wish what happened to me as a kid on anyone else. I am thankful that I saw a way *out* of the darkness and self-sabotage. What happened to me as a kid made me *stronger,* but more importantly *healthier.*

May this book help you become *stronger.*
May this book help you become *healthier.*
May this book help you *stop the destruction.*
May this book help you *into wholeness.*

About The Author

Jason Thompson is a happily married man and father of four. He is a firm believer in the Lord and son of God. Jason is a Massage Therapist, Founder of MyaTherapy, Creator of the Body Mapping System, and a two time published author. During his 34 years of life, he has been on a mission to help people heal and get out of pain through the power of consistency; so they can step into their greatness and experience the results they desire. Jason grew up in Colorado and currently resides there with his family.

Jason strongly believes men are designed for great things in life, yet a man cannot truly become the great man he was destined to be if he has not healed from childhood traumas. Healing from molestation and sex addiction has allowed Jason to operate in his genuine authenticity.

When we have men who are not operating from fear and trauma, our families and community reap all the benefits. Healthier men mean healthier families and communities.

If this book has touched your life, or you would like to contact the author for a speaking invitation, please send an email to KingJason10M@gmail.com.

Made in the USA
Middletown, DE
16 February 2021